Dreamtelling

Focus on Contemporary Issues (FOCI) addresses the pressing problems, ideas and debates of the new millennium. Subjects are drawn from the arts, sciences and humanities, and are linked by the impact they have had or are having on contemporary culture. FOCI books are intended for an intelligent, alert audience with a general understanding of, and curiosity about, the intellectual debates shaping culture today. Instead of easing readers into a comfortable awareness of particular fields, these books are combative. They offer points of view, take sides and are written with passion.

SERIES EDITORS
Barrie Bullen and Peter Hamilton

In the same series

Cool Rules
Dick Pountain and David Robins

Chromophobia
David Batchelor

Global Dimensions
John Rennie Short

Celebrity
Chris Rojek

Activism!
Tim Jordan

Animal
Erica Fudge

Dreamtelling

PIERRE SORLIN

REAKTION BOOKS

Published by Reaktion Books Ltd
79 Farringdon Road
London EC1M 3JU, UK

www.reaktionbooks.co.uk

First published 2003

Series design by Libanus Press
Printed and bound in Great Britain by
Biddles Ltd, Guildford and King's Lynn

British Library Cataloguing in Publishing Data
Sorlin, Pierre
    Dreamtelling. – (FOCI)
    1. Dreams 2. Dream interpretation
    I. Title
    154.6'3

ISBN 1 86189 150 4

Contents

Introduction

The word *dream* is often used to refer to something that does not exist in the present. It is a hope, a wish, a longing. I can *dream* of climbing Everest or winning a Nobel prize, but I know such achievements are beyond me. Other challenges are achievable, however; they can become reality. We often say we are dreaming when completely absorbed in our own thoughts. On a gloomy November day, for example, I might fancy what it would be like to spend my summer holiday on a sunny beach. I am daydreaming. Dreams embody the mind's power to imagine what we would like to happen. Twice, first in the *Republic* then in the *Laws*, Plato sketches out the best possible city, an ideal association of body and head, the 'pure creation of our dreams'. Such utopias – of which 'the American Dream' may be the ultimate version – include a visionary idea of the future greatness of a perfect commonwealth, a country offering unlimited possibilities. Such dreams are not irrational: they involve logical thoughts.

Nightdreams

But *dream* is generally used with rather a different meaning. It desig-
nates the train of thoughts, images and sensations that occur in the
mind during sleep. Some dreams are highly visual. Others have virtually
no visual content. Some dreams are comforting, others can fill one with
despair. We are overwhelmed by what Wordsworth, remembering his
Paris nightmares in the tenth book of *The Prelude*, named 'ghastly
visions of despair'; or, on the contrary, as Coleridge wrote to his friend
Robert Southey, we can 'attain a kind of visual magnificence with a
correspondent intensity of general feeling'.[1] Occasionally, while asleep,
we are absolutely certain we have understood something important. A
difficult problem, or perhaps the meaning of life itself, is now perfectly
clear. We believe that, later, we shall make the best of such a revelation.
Such experiences are in fact mere impressions, the consequence of an
emotional, euphoric state of mind, and they dissolve when we wake up:
'Then all the charm / Is broken – all that phantom-world so fair /
Vanishes, and a thousand circlets spread . . .', as Coleridge says in 'The
Picture'.

A Dream

'*In a corner of the room are three black silhouettes. Men, surely.
They have no face or personality. They are waiting for me, I should
take them somewhere. I am wearing my dressing-gown, I must have
a shower. Now there is another person, a woman, she is wearing a
tartan jacket and glasses. She must be in her thirties. They all look
impatient but I can't have my shower here, while she's present, I
must go to an external bathroom. There are bathrooms in the corridor; there, on the right. I am going along the corridor, it's the
Bodleian library, I pass many young people. There are wonderful*

paintings on the walls, I should stop to look at them but I remember I did it some time ago. There are no bathrooms, only small studies. I turn right. I am still walking, it's a beach, we go along the shore, there are children with me. We are approaching a big detached house. I ask the lady: "Is this yours?" She points to a wall: "No, mine is there."

We do not know the name of this dreamer. We cannot even tell whether it is a woman or a man. Yet the content of the dream seems familiar. Who has not dreamed of wearing light clothes while among well-dressed people, of resisting an insistent demand to get out, of pacing a long corridor, of walking on the sea-shore? Every moment of this dream seems the beginning of a short story. As Kafka noted in his *Diaries*, a simple sentence that starts a tale can conjure up an entire world in our imagination.

The variety of hypotheses propounded from Antiquity to the present day proves that dreams do not lend themselves to a definitive, wholly satisfying explanation. Many dream theories are thought-provoking. We owe much to Freud and Jung, in particular, because they have drawn our attention to unnoticed aspects of our dreams and have prevented us from indulging in simplistic explanations. But Freud's and Jung's ideas are incompatible, and any attempt to find an all-encompassing explanation seems delusory. Dreaming deals at once with many different things; unrelated details are drawn into an image or into a series of visual and sensual perceptions that do not follow the logical order of daytime fantasies. For that reason dreams are not easily explained to others. When a person attempts to report a dream, his or her mind is awash with other matters – memories, fantasies, desires, anxieties, stray associations, acts of censorship and substitution. Would it not be reasonable to assume that dreaming is a wholly private, first-person experience and, as such, a subject that falls within the category of individual psychology? Yet, by insisting that dreams are explicable, psychoanalysists attempt interpretation. For them, an individual's life experiences result in dreams containing meanings that relate to that life.

Ancient Egyptians, Greeks and Arabs were long bent on gathering information on dreams, but it was only in the 1950s that systematic investigations began when Professor Kleitman and Dr Aserinsky at the University of Chicago noticed that their patients' eyes moved during sleep. Electrodes placed close to the patients' eyes and connected to electroencephalographs allowed them to detect various stages of sleep. Far from evolving progressively from slumber to deep sleep, a night is divided into short sequences of, alternately, light and deep sleep. The former are accompanied by quick eye movements; the latter by slow movements, so that sleep has since been conventionally divided between periods of REM (rapid eye movement) and NREM (non-rapid eye movement). REM sleep was labelled 'paradoxical', because during this phase the body is at its most relaxed, whereas the brain is active. Rigorous sampling has shown that during this period dreams are particularly intense and hallucinatory, although dream-like thoughts occur, if less frequently, in other moments of sleep, known as 'orthodox' sleep. REM and NREM phases happen in turn during the night; the REM states usually add up to about 90 minutes per night. It has been calculated that, in an average person's lifetime, around six years are spent in dreaming. Yet most dreams are not remembered when one awakes. Only occasionally do we recall fragments of our dreams, often because of their striking content.

In the 1960s Dr W. C. Dement, working with American volunteers, woke his volunteers every time they entered a stage of REM; he observed that as soon as they were left in peace, they fell back into REM sleep and dreamed. If the experiment was prolonged over several days the subjects were seriously perturbed, while other volunteers woken only during NREM sleep were tired but not disturbed. Dement's conclusion was that dreaming is not a casual, negligible activity, but a vital bodily function. Since sleeping dogs and cats twitch in sleep and move their eyes, it is sometimes claimed that a number of higher animals dream. But the deep nature of dreams still eludes scientific explanation; a gap lies between our subjective experience and any possible objective explanation.

Dreams, Culture and Society

And yet, dreams are not necessarily mysterious, nor do they comprise only personal problems. They are linked not just to imaginary but also to perfectly existing circumstances, and, more importantly, to aspects of the surrounding world. They deal with issues such as work, wages, leisure – all concerning both the group and the individual. In addition, different people can dream of the same fact or situation. This seems to show that our dreams lie partly beyond the boundaries of our experience. During the Great War of 1914–18, soldiers of both sides living in trenches at the Front and under constant threaten of sudden death were experiencing exactly the same types of dream. An important question is therefore the conditions during which we have various dreams as well as the situations that produce them. Culture – interpreted here as attitudes, behaviour, values and traditions shared in various social groups – is a relevant aspect of our imagination. That we depend on our environment cannot be contested, though it is worth recalling that the very nature of many mental states, including the generation of images while sleeping, presupposes a relation to our environment.

Since dreams are social and cultural phenomena, there are two ways of questioning their social basis. First we could take into account the mental habits and expectations of various cultural communities, how they differentiate dreams from other conscious or unconscious activities, such as will, fantasy, memory, insanity. Let us consider an example of difference. According to Muhammad's revelations collected in the *Koran,* there is no clear-cut distinction between dream and vision. Both may be aural or visual experiences. Their mystical value depends on the visionary's moral and religious preparedness. But in the Hindi tradition the world is considered a mere illusion, an image dreamed by the deity; human beings wander through semblances. Only when dreaming do they have access to the cosmic plan and gain an insight into reality. Dreams are windows opening on to a truth more universal and authentic than material appearances. Thus distinct understandings regarding dreams and dreaming coexist in the Indian subcontinent, where Muslims and Hindis live together. According to the former, the right to relate and interpret a mental intuition is the privilege of a blessed minority. According to the latter, all who have the potential to become yogis, thanks to ascetic observances and meditation, enter into a state of conscious dreaming. We could easily catalogue other spiritual frameworks, classify dreams according to their context, and use the results for comparative research. However, this might 'freeze' the notion of culture and lead us to forget that customs are in constant flux. In the Middle Ages Muslim exegetes distinguished dreams where lesser prophets received messages transmitted by God from wakening visions reserved for greater prophets. The nature of the perception that helped to measure the dignity of blessedness was more important than its content.

Both dreams and theories, the object of interpreters' explanations, are obviously influenced by the context in which the dreamers live – by objects, buildings, landscapes and even trivia familiar to them and contemporary events that affect their lives. Another approach would be to follow, from the ancient world to our own, the successive frameworks of dream elucidation. In any historical period, a dominant system of thought, whether religious or scientific, gives unity to the modes of knowledge. Dreams are formed within the context of a cultural background. Such knowledge might help us to understand how people in different epochs conceived of dreams, how they told them and what images they 'saw' while asleep. In the mental representations of ancient, polytheistic societies, deities were superhuman powers or creatures capable of interfering in human existence. Most Greeks endowed entities like dreams with a personality and believed that, while asleep, their bodies were permeable to cosmic forces. In *The Iliad* (II, 5), Zeus sends Agamemnon a dream that is at the same time the *messenger* bearing the dream: 'The dream departs at Zeus' word; swift he flies down to where the Achaean ships lie, goes to Agamemnon's camp and tells him . . .'. This materialistic view was not universal, but those who failed to share it nevertheless treated dreams as independent entities. According to Plato (*Phaedo*, 60, e), Socrates mentioned a dream that 'visited' him repeatedly, 'always saying the same things'. The biblical and neo-biblical, that is, the Judaeo-Christian and the Islamic worlds, did not attribute to dreams a semi-bodily presence, but understood them as messages sent directly from God or Satan. During the European Age of Modernity, roughly from the fifteenth century to the nineteenth, there was a sense of a united self, whose identity and introspective capacity implied a continuity between waking and sleeping life. 'I Dreamt a Dream! / what can it mean?' asked William Blake in 'The Angel', one of his *Songs of Experience*; his answer emphasized the relevance of the personal agency in dream development; his comforting vision symbolized the enthusiasm aroused by youth, so that dreams ceased once 'the time of youth was fled / And grey hairs were on my head'. Nineteenth-century Positivism, instead of considering dreams as a process apt to throw light on individual thoughts, encouraged interest in theorizing about their relation to physiology. Dreaming, like any other function, had to be deciphered since it was likely to divulge information regarding mental sanity. Positivism revived the study of dreams in medical and scientific circles. Many important books were written on the subject, but my view is that they were dealing mainly with analytical issues, cautiously describing clinical cases, and avoiding the temptation to construct grand theories. A few scientists, impressed by the random character of dreams, put forward – against the idea of the unity of the self – the hypothesis of a duality between the conscious and the unconscious. What was the origin of the unconscious? Was it purely mental or was it physiological? Physiologists and psychologists quarrelled bitterly until Freud suggested that dreams were wish-fulfilments, or messages from our unconscious. Freud's *The Interpretation of Dreams* (1900) changed the terms of the debate, for it was a presentation of broad principles for the whole psychic structure of human beings (in fact, mostly Western men), together with a complex methodology to understand dreams. The book soon became a classic, and everyone had their views about dreams along with a set of principles to defend them and a theoretical model to justify them.

Attempts to explain dreams have always been a source of vigorous controversy, and it would not be difficult to follow the historical development of these debates. However, history is the study of significant changes; it focuses on the transition from one system to another, whether intellectual, political or economic. Are we in a position to maintain that dreaming has been evolving for centuries? We are encouraged to believe that only in recent times has direct observation taken over from received wisdom, whereas in fact ancient commentators anticipated contemporary scientific techniques. Waking sleepers immediately after they seem to have been dreaming in order to ask them to report their experience was a method known in antiquity. It is mentioned in *Gilgamesh*, a Babylonian epic preserved on clay tablets that date from the third millennium BC. In ancient Mesopotamia and Greece, those who slept in sanctuaries in order to receive divine messages had to be woken immediately after the disappearance of the heavenly emissary. Alert inquirers have long observed a nocturnal dream cycle. In his accurate study of sleep, Synesius, a Roman landowner, later bishop of Cyrene at the beginning of the fourth century AD, distinguished the lightest stage of sleep preceding awakening, characterized by swift dreams, almost real, from a former, much deeper sleep.[2] Tertullian, an early Christian theologian (third century AD), linked dream content to the sleeper's mental and physical condition.[3] In the same way, another careful observer, Macrobius, who lived in the fourth century AD, noted that there were different periods of sleep, notably what he called 'the first cloud of sleep', when people do not understand that they are slipping into sleep yet who are already dreaming.[4] Obviously, in ancient times no careful measurements were undertaken, and the observations were not as precise as those we gain from encephalography, but the ancients knew perfectly well that there are different phases of sleep.

There have always been different frameworks of dream interpretation, often at variance with one another, but far from coming to light successively, they do in fact *coexist*. Mixing up 'popular' beliefs and more elaborate or scientific evaluations help accommodate recurring images, already found in ancient texts, with new curiosities. In our own, so-called 'rational' times, when everyone is aware of the basic theories of psychoanalysis, dreambooks (books of dream divination) sell well. Those that buy them think that dreams will enable them to probe their unconscious and, at the same time, hope that somehow, while asleep, they will be told the next winning lottery number. A few details included in dreams are obviously linked to the historical context. Nobody before the twentieth century dreamed they were in an aeroplane. However, aeroplanes in dreams are no more than mental representations of internal sensations previously converted into different images. Ancient Greek or Roman manuals explaining how to decipher dreams often mention dreams where people have the impression they are flying or floating in the air. In our own day dreams of flying don't always involve aeroplanes. Countless references to the contemporary world that surface in dreams concern us, and I will deal with them at length. But, in the background, there is also that accumulation of persistent features found in different periods.

One Thousand and One Nights

Echoes and reappearances make dreams additionally fascinating. A few elements standing for a limited number of basic aspects of human existence, such as birth, sex and death, seem to have been held in common by dreamers of all times. How can we be certain of that? Thanks to the fact that dreamtelling has long been a characteristic of human culture. For example, it is recorded in the Bible that Daniel 'had a dream and visions of his head upon his bed: then he wrote [down] the dream' (Daniel, 7, 1). People ranging from William Laud and Elias Ashmole in the seventeenth century, Robert Southey and John Ruskin in the nineteenth, and later the Austrian playwright Arthur Schnitzler, Franz Kafka, Katherine Mansfield, Graham Greene, Carl Jung and even Freud himself – all of them noted down what they had dreamed. Hundreds of anonymous people have sent accounts of their dreams to newspapers, recorded them in their diaries, shared them with doctors, psychiatrists and investigators only too happy to transcribe them in their books or papers.[5] Dreams have often been passed around like news. We are told in Genesis (37, 5–6) that 'Joseph dreamed a dream, and he told *it* [to] his brethren. . . . And he said unto them, Hear, I pray you, this dream which I have dreamed'; in Jeremiah (23, 27) there is a reference to the dreams that people have 'which they tell every man to his neighbour'. Guides to divination containing precise examples of dreams date from ancient Egypt. One of the most elaborate, the Chester Beatty Papyrus, was compiled more than 3,000 years ago. Later, Artemidorius of Ephesus's *Oneirocriticon* ('The Interpretation of Dreams'), written in the mid-second century AD, has been pirated or imitated by countless other manuals right up to the present day. Coleridge's correspondence reveals an active exchange of dream reports within his intellectual circle. For instance, he thanked his patron Thomas Poole for an account that, having been circulated to various friends, 'has been greatly admired' and spoken of 'in high commendation'. On another occasion Coleridge confessed that the theme of *The Rhyme of the Ancient Mariner* was borrowed from a strange vision recounted by a friend. In addition to direct or indirect reports, we have a great number of dreams in literature and art. No less than 43 are mentioned in the Old Testament, five in the Gospel According to Matthew, four in the Acts of the Apostles. Biblical dreams have been an inexhaustible source of inspiration for artists, Rembrandt's *The Angel Appearing to St Joseph in his Dream* being but one among a myriad of related works. Many of Shakespeare's plays, Pedro Calderón's *Life is a Dream*, Charles Dickens's *A Christmas Carol*, Nerval's *Aurélia*, countless Romantic poems, Coleridge's *Kubla Khan*, Keats's *La Belle Dame sans Merci*, Wordsworth's *The Prelude* use the dream as a counterpoint to actual life. And cinema was quick to take advantage of the 'pictorial' aspect of dreaming.

There is much source material, even though it is rather patchy. How can it be explored, given the variations in the nature and amount of information available and its limited reliability? How would it be possible to use – simultaneously – dreams recorded in the lives of saints or prophets, those contrived by poets, those printed in books on medicine and those told by the dreamers themselves? Only the last named seem faithful, or at least superior to, memories communicated by an indirect witness, and far more reliable than literary dreams in poems and novels or in sacred texts like the Bible. And yet these 'direct' accounts are not scientific protocols but mere attempts to retain fading memories. Since it reconfigures what was briefly perceived and explores the limits of what is expressible, the dreamtelling process essentially must be of a fragile nature. It is also a risky affair, like any private subject-matter, since revealing one's dreams could easily be considered a form of exhibitionism. In addition, many reports may have been reworked by the dreamer, either to dress them up or to conceal embarrassing details.

Dreamtelling is concerned with what has been written or said about dreams. My aim is not to 'interpret' dreams, to attempt to explain their hidden meaning or to identify the part of the 'message' that concerns the dreamer's personal fate, but to look for systematic relationships among the diverse ways dreams have long been told, analyzed and explained. In this respect, even indirect information has something to tell us. Regarding St Augustine's reports of his mother's dreams, we may doubt the accuracy of his description. Nevertheless, it reveals what a Christian allowed herself to fancy in the fourth century AD, and how the same dreams were diversely interpreted by an ageing woman and her young son. Similarly, manuals of dream interpretation, trotting out the same classifications since Artemidorius, adapt their exegesis to the spirit of their times. The examples given in them are simplified versions of dreams reported to the interpreters by their clients, and as such tell us which types of dream were the most common and how they were understood. 'Literary' dreams seem less serviceable, since most writers, instead of aiming to transcribe the actual experience of dreaming, make great efforts to shape the dreams to the stories' artistic requirements. However, plays, novels and, above all, those poems that take liberties with the order of time and space involve the production of images, colour combinations, associations of words and fantastic elements consonant with the capricious, sometimes enigmatic, blossoming of dreams.

Medical or psychological essays present a more difficult problem. Based on observations or discussions with dreamers and investigations into their past, they are thought to be scientific. Yet, we should be wary of the difference between factual findings and interpretations. Following the experimental observations mentioned earlier, it has been suggested that dreams where we believe we are flying are related to organic events, especially to bodily movements made while asleep to keep ourselves comfortable in bed. Such a statement can be checked, possibly modified, even refuted, and, in this respect, it is scientific. However, it does not explain why some patients fly by means of wings, others travel in aeroplanes and still others float about without knowing how. Interpretations are not amenable to the same testing as observations are. In order to make sense of visions and recollections as fleeting as those in dreams, specialists need a theoretical framework that will make rational discussion possible. Such underlying assumptions cannot be controlled. They are neither true nor false, but they are indispensable, though, in many cases, they are not particularly convincing, and often they are even slightly odd. If there were no theories, everything in dreams would look extravagant, they would simply be individual delusions, and therefore not to be taken seriously. It could be argued that the phenomena that occur while people are asleep are meaningless. Yet, for millennia, people have endeavoured to find meaning in them. Even soothsayers like Artemidorius believed in the consistent, everyday nature of dreaming and sought to define laws, however puerile they may seem to us. Medical or scientific interpretations are discourses, and, as such, are part of the numerous views, opinions or beliefs that have been expressed about dreams.

Despite cautious methods of inquiry, the facts already known about dreams are understood by neurologists and psychologists in fairly different, often conflicting ways. Some scientists conceive of dreams as cleansing operations: the brain rids itself of useless accumulated daytime information. Others contend that dreams help us to remain vigilant or are provoked by certain reactions in brain cells. However, the most widely popular current theory is psychoanalysis. Included in 'folk psychology', many of psychoanalysis's major tenets are part of the way we understand ourselves and each other. Its vocabulary has spread through all strata and developed into a common idiom for behaviour at both the individual and collective level. The status of psychoanalysis has consequences for many aspects of social and intellectual life in the West. We would all go on dreaming if psychoanalysis collapsed, but not entirely in the same way. Psychoanalytic theory, or central aspects of it, are deeply embedded in shared common sense. For that reason psychoanalysis is not simply a matter of concern within scientific circles, it has practical consequences for the way dreamers conceive of their dreams, interpret them and tell them. Although Freud's theories lie at the heart of all modern interpretive advances in the field, psychoanalysis must not be mistaken for Freudianism. Many analysts admit that dreams introduce us to a better understanding of the unconscious, but question Freud's interpretations, or at least consider that no one is in a position to test their truthfulness.

If psychoanalysis has provided a new framework for the debate regarding the significance of dreams, it has not solved the enigma of their origin. Controversies continue concerning the purely psychological or predominantly neurological aspects of dreams. In addition to medicine, a wide range of philosophical frames of study is involved in the debate. Epistemological questions (how do I know that I am not dreaming now, as I write?), and metaphysical ones (how do I know whether the whole of my life is nothing but a dream?) surfaced during the seventeenth century and are still associated with the study of dreams.

In *Dreamtelling* I will not be considering issues related to the philosophy of knowledge, neurophysiology or analysis. What I want to explore are the discourses that people have produced and are still generating about an activity common to all of us, the way dreams have become an object of intellectual speculation. Dreams are fancies that take place in an individual's head, but what appears to be a private game is, at the same time, a universal game in which everyone participates, a form of imagining that is common to mankind. But the very stuff of dreams slips from our waking minds. What we grasp afterwards are not images or sounds but the interaction of what we remember with the ways that dreamtelling happens in society. My enquiry will be essentially qualitative, in my effort to evaluate the most persistent aspects of dreaming, and how dreams have been told and interpreted through the centuries. In other words, *Dreamtelling* is an attempt to consider dreams from a cross-cultural, anthropological point of view.

Perhaps dreams have always perplexed and fascinated people because they are so mysterious, combining precise images and vague impressions, or, as Coleridge found in 'The Pains of Sleep', in dreams 'Desire with loathing [is] strangely mixed'. Dreaming is a paradoxical activity. It is relatively easy to describe what we think we have seen or heard in sleep, but attempts to convey kinetic sensations or pure thrills are doomed to failure. Is this not the reason why people have long been, and are still, speculating about their dreams? To try to penetrate a mystery that cannot be expressed in any language seems at one and the same time to be both challenging and hopeless.

Dreaming has often been compared to a cinema of the mind that switches on periodically. Since dreams subvert rational behaviour and routines of the day with experiences on the wilder shores of existence, they have always triggered the imagination. Writers and artists have always used them to create fanciful worlds unfettered by earthly limitations. The purpose of Chapter One is not to list the various accounts of the meaning of dreams, but to see how the idea of the other reality they suggest has been used and transformed by imaginative individuals.

Why do we dream? Chapter Two does not attempt to answer the question, nor is it a summary of dream theories. Its aim is to dig out the religious, philosophical or scientific assumptions that are the bases of these schemes. A scrutiny of various texts shows that, despite their diversity, they all try to tackle the same problem: what do dreams tell us about human nature?

There are many ways of conceiving of the nature of dreams. What accounts for the differences? Chapter Three suggests that to a large extent it is the way the story is told. There is a paradox concerning a psychic event as important as a dream: a dream is never afterwards known *as it really happened*, not even by the dreamer himself: the dream can only be told *after* the dreamer has woken up. The dreamtelling – with all the limits imposed by memory, expression and repetition – makes sense of the sequence of images that the dreamer remembers by linking them; and explains why, when they are recounted, dreams usually find an eager audience.

The interpretation of dreams has seldom been taken from theological or psychological sources alone, but has always involved more factual considerations, giving relative weight to certain aspects of contemporary life and not to others. Chapter Four contends that there is little truth, or direct information, about any one era to be uncovered in these fantasies; current problems or fashions have always been treated simply as figures capable of a range of emotions, changing and developing according to the dreamer's situation. Dream content consists of personal and interpersonal or social data interpreted personally. The selection of basic elements and the images it produces help us to recover anxieties, values and references found in human society at a given time.

At the end of the night, dreams do not speak for themselves. They are only heard when expressed through ideas and frames of reference understood by both the dream interpreters and their audiences. Hence the power acquired by those who are considered able to 'translate' dreams. Chapter Five will explore the longlasting popularity of explanations, ranging from the commonsensical to the most sophisticated.

CHAPTER ONE

Dreams and Imagination

The nineteenth-century doctors and psychologists who launched systematic investigations into dreams sought to develop a scientific theory of them. Laboratory experiences led the clinicians to dismiss the enigmatic content of these delusions and to focus on purely biological factors, such as the successive periods of sleep. As for the psychotherapists, they used dream reports to help their clients relax and talk when when they were reluctant to expose their problems. Before Freud the stories we fantasize at night were often an object of scorn, partly because they could not be measured and classified but also because they were considered a source of superstition and fallacy.

Scholarly dream investigation began while the Europeans, embarked on the sharing out of Africa and Asia, were exploring the customs of 'uncivilized' parts of the world. Ethnography was a derivative of colonization, the learned community bringing itself up to date on 'primitive' beliefs, and Freud and Jung found in ethnographic writings arguments for their assumptions about the human mind's primary process. In the light of biological discoveries the speculations on divine revelation transmitted during sleep seemed childish. Such myths were attributed to the dependence on natural factors. Not surprisingly, tribes plunged in darkness at night could take dream figures for real people, but such confusion was impossible in the age of electricity.

As heirs to twentieth-century rationalist thinkers our contemporaries do not overvalue dreams. Other cultures and periods took sleeping life more seriously. The clear distinction we make between waking and dreaming is still irrelevant in pre-industrial societies, where observing the outer world, having visions and dreaming are often seen as one continuum. What is underestimated in many modern theories is the purely emotional aspect of dreams deriving from the transformation of motivations, relationships, ideas into shapes, colours, figures or ill-defined elements. Sceptical though we are regarding the importance of our visions, we happen to be affected during sleep by intensely joyful or distressing feelings provoked by an inside impression or by a strange apparition, by curious circumstances, by an incomprehensible combination of images. Feeding human fantasy dreams have long contributed to expand creativity. It is their stimulating, image-provoking power we shall explore in this chapter.

Wandering Souls

We are used to calling 'objective', things or people we perceive when we focus our attention on them. Since we cannot control our dreams, and since they appear or vanish autonomously, we consider them subjective. But is it always easy to make a distinction between internal and external experiences? First World War veterans who had met hell in the trenches kept encountering dead bodies imploring not to be buried; they saw undertakers' assistants ready to bury them with the corpses; awaking in panic they realized they had dreamed and were repeating the horrible scenes they had experienced at the Front. Traumatic dreams,[1] it will be argued, must be considered exceptional and not probative. So let us take another example.

> 'I was seated in the drawing-room, facing the window. Someone entered the room and crept toward me. I was frightened, but I wanted neither to turn round nor to run away. Then a tall, dark man was in front of me. He came close to me, put his hand on my head, then showed me the window. I awoke, shivering and in a sweat. I knew Death had really stared me in the face.'

It was a subjective vision, but so vivid that the man apprehended it like an actual happening. But he may have been feverish and inclined to confuse facts and fancies. Let us examine a much commoner case. Many have in mind the sharp picture of a landscape, a street, a silhouette, a face but do not know whether they actually saw it in a place they do not remember or whether it was a dream. Dream images not especially strange or exceptional often make a strong impression on the sleeper.

The cases we have mentioned are personalized and unique. How does a transition occur from an individual vision to a collective belief in the corporeality of dream figures? Let us return to the pre-radio and television period. In many villages or in large families people used to assemble at dusk to listen to stories. When there were no more tales, they told each other their dreams, and the best storytellers embellished theirs, making it sound like an invented fable. Victor Hugo was especially good at this game, and his dream accounts illustrate the power of creative imagination. In July 1842, Ferdinand d'Orléans, the eldest son of Louis-Philippe, was killed in a street accident. As heir to the throne of France his death made a strong impression. Shortly after, in a dream, Hugo received the duke's visit. What is striking in the account he wrote in his memoirs[2] is less the meeting than the scenery. Hugo recreated – during sleep? or merely in his report? the question is irrelevant, all we have is the written account – a remarkable atmosphere similar in aspect to the environment he was evoking, at the same time, in his poems.

'I was at home, but this home was not mine, I do not know it. There were several huge lounges, very beautiful and much lit. That was in the evening. A summer night. I was in a lounge, beside a table, with my friends, my dream friends, all unknown to me. We were happily talking and heartily laughing. The windows were wide open. The duke entered the room. We sat, the duke and I, near a window opening on an admirable view. That was in a city. In my dream I was familiar with the city, but in fact I did not know it. Beyond the window there lay, extending very far, between two massive structures of buildings, a wide river brightly moon lit in some of its parts. In the background, in the mist, stayed the two sharp, huge towers of some extraordinary cathedral. On the left, near the window, our view lost its way in a dark alley. I do not remember, in the city, any window lights nor any inhabitants in the streets . . . The sky was pastel blue and charmingly soft. In a corner a mild wind was stirring hardly visible trees. The river murmured gently. Everything radiated I do not know what inexpressible serenity. It was like feeling the soul of things.'

Hugo's account is suggestive, at times fanciful, at times precise. Let us risk an hypothesis. Imagine that Hugo had told his grandchildren his vision. How many of them would have firmly believed that the Duke, shortly before his death, had paid a visit to the great man? Let us go a bit further. During winter nights, people gathering around the fireplace improvised stories; dreams and traditional tales mixed easily. Dreams are a good device for introducing fairies or other fantastic beings in a fable. For instance, in the Grimm brothers' collection, the protagonists, while asleep, receive useful information or have their work completed by mysterious, dream-like spirits.

But such compilations, being the learned version of popular tales, distinguish radically a human, a possible world from a magical or mythical one. In these legends the nocturnal ghosts are ephemeral partners who vanish as fast as they emerge and do not interfere in the heroes' worldly destiny. If we want to meet chimeras likely to materialize during sleep we must travel to another cultural world. In a television report on Cambodia filmed in 1999, a pregnant woman spoke of her dreams.[3] A few notes about the context are necessary. Following her husband, who was digging trenches for an industrial company, the woman had left her village and settled in a zone where hundreds had been killed during the civil war. The day before the filming, the husband had dug up a human bone, and the woman, deeply scared, decided to go for comfort to the local healer. In the film she tells him: 'Since I have been here I have not had good dreams. I only dream of cruel ghosts. There is a big, menacing one. He is in love with me, he wants to marry me. I do not want. My husband and I have burnt incense.' The healer answers slowly and does not get directly to the point. He evokes the countless casualties, the dead who having not been properly buried cannot be reincarnated. They wander, haunting the living. 'They want to marry you, or to catch and kill you, to drown you.'

The dialogue takes place in the sphere of uncertain belief. The woman wonders whether her ghost was an illusion or a real visitor, but she is not looking for a clear-cut answer, such as yes or no. The healer is cautious not to be be too precise. Like many Cambodians he thinks that everything has a soul – having a soul being any existence's correlate – and that homeless spirits in search of a place to stay assail sleepers. Is there a ghost bent on marrying the woman? Or is she upset by her exile, her pregnancy, the risk run by her husband when he digs soil filled with undefused bombs?

We are used to conceiving of dreams as separate from active life, but there are cultures where such dissociation is meaningless. The dialogue between the Cambodians discloses the absence of certainty in this field. Dreamed creatures have a substance of their own not comparable to human or animal flesh. Arizonian Indians – Navajos and Yumas – are accustomed to deadly invitation spectres. During sleep they can hear a voice, someone or something calls and tries to lure them into the underworld: the ground opens before them, they follow a path that ends at an abyss. They resist, they cling to the edge, they run away. When they get out they understand they have escaped from a death valley.

Any attempt to expound what is felt or believed by the sleepers is futile; there is no doctrine, merely an acceptance of a shared creed. An estrangement from one's own body during sleep is a common event. Isolde Kurtz, who liked to report her dreams, noted for instance: 'In my vision I make plans for a trip where my body will hamper me. Therefore I leave without it and let it stay in my bed. Later I happen to go past it and I examine it. It is flat like an empty goatskin.'[4] Phantasmagorical for a young German lady, such a delusion was, and is still, taken seriously in pre-industrial societies, where it is meant to prove the reality of an autonomous, not corporeal activity. Here comes the soul, a vital principle, bound and not bound to a person, independent but weak and endangered when it is not incarnate. The notion of spirit is closely linked to the dreamers' daily remembrance and to the types of dream acceptable in a community. In return, the community's conception of soul feeds back into, and modifies, the content of dreams. The Mongolian Buryats, who are shamanist hunters, think that an alliance with the forest spirit is essential for the driving out and killing of animals. The spirit's daughter appears and guides the hunter. She happens to fall in love with this man and visits him during sleep. Their affair must be confined to an hallucinated intercourse. If the hunter sought a fleshly encounter with the daughter, he would run into the forest, go berserk and die. No one would attempt to save him.[5] Hunting rituals, forest legends or beliefs, and actual dreams mix up and reinforce one other.

The main point is the soul's freedom in sleep. Such conviction is attested in the tradition of numerous societies. Four thousand years ago the Egyptians associated sleep with death, the former being considered the latter's passing anticipation. At night the sleeper's spirit was meant to travel to parts of the Underworld. In other communities the dreamer's soul is supposed to take advantage of its liberation; the dreams are its journeys through faraway landscapes, its visits to ancestors, its meetings with other souls.

Such peregrinations are not harmless. The vagrant spirit of an unburied corpse can enter a sleeper's empty body. What is worse, the wandering soul may be attacked by another, more combative, soul. St Theodore Tyron's Greek legend in its tenth-century version[6] provides a good example of just such a perilous encounter. Theodore and other knights were summoned by the emperor, who had been attacked, during sleep, by a man of the highest standing, dark faced and carrying two bows. 'He assaulted me, pierced me, broke my limbs.' The emperor's words were unequivocal: there had been a battle between souls, the emperor had lost, his spirit had been crushed and he was in danger of his life. Theodore, after a long quest, found the man in Syria, caught him and brought him to the emperor, who had him executed. What we call nightmare has long been in different cultures a terrific and undoubtedly risky ordeal. When Euripides in *Hecuba* (71–72), addressing the 'mother of the dusk-winged dreams that fly around' urged 'the sinister vision of darkness to go away', he did not merely keep away an unpleasant vision but repelled an actual menace.

The vagabond spirit may return too late if the sleeper is awakened abruptly, or, if having found a more pleasant place to stay, it is not in a hurry to come back. The sleeper is then risking death. George the Monk's ninth-century chronicle mentions the case of an African soldier who died, was buried but, once in his grave, shouted so loudly that his grave was opened and he was found alive.[7] He explained how his soul had undergone a typical vision of Hell. At the end of his exploration 'I saw my fetid and dark body and I said I could not revert to it', but having to choose between Hell, in punishment for his sins, and Resurrection, he preferred the latter. Reluctant spirits must sometimes be pursued. Soul-seekers can be found among Chaco Indians, New Guinea Papuans and Siberians. The soul hunting takes the form of a ritual, and, at the end, the searcher reports the dreamed itinerary he has covered during sleep.

Eleven centuries separate George the Monk and Isolde Kurtz, but both used the same image of a derelict body and described the emancipated spirit's boundless odyssey. Many features of dreams are timeless, and the reports delivered in daytime are a way of ordering the dreams' varied facets in the framework of one's culture: the Christian faith for the monk, world-wide travelling for a twentieth-century young woman. This explains why we cannot ask if Siberians, Indians or Papuans believe in their vision's truth. Their account is delivered within their culture's conceptual system, with reference to learned, internalized beliefs; it talks about that culture and contributes to reinforce it. Most individuals distinguish their dreams from waking action, but they are also able to combine dreams and daytime thoughts and to make dreams elements of their relationship with their social and natural surroundings. In such contexts, dreaming and dreamtelling are emotional experiences; they arouse both in the narrator and the listeners tangled and conflicting feelings of kinds sufficient to confirm the importance of dreams in the life of the community.

Life as it is in Our Dreams

Dreams do not mean for us what they do for a Siberian shaman. Have we lost a deep, vivid language that is now only preserved in small, traditional groups? Recurrent complaints concerning the uniformity brought about by modernity – an ill-defined word – stress the devaluation of dreams in the contemporary world. We are absorbed, it is said, by our earthly affairs; our narrow, busy minds have become unable to picture the infinity only dreams could allow our spirit to develop and explore freely.

The members of some pre-industrial communities seem capable of entering another, ideal realm during sleep, but none of them will certify that this world is richer, more spiritual than their ordinary surroundings. Information on the topic is imprecise not because people do not want to talk, but because they have difficulty in accounting for their dreams. A Cambodian working in Europe explains how, in his country, he believes in the soul's multiplicity and in the spirit's migration through dreams, but dismisses such convictions as soon as he arrives in the West.

Not all pre-industrial communities move nimbly between dreaming and waking. According to the Australian Aborigines, in the age of The Dreaming, an era antecedent to the present epoch, earth was inhabited by the Ancestors born from the dream and represented on rupestrian, self-created paintings. These were actual but dreamed beings who understood nature's language and created rituals out of their visions. People have lost such limitless communication with the universe, but it may fleetingly be restored during sleep. The spirit, the Mardudjara of Western Australia contend, can leave the body during dreams, return to ancestral places and perform rituals necessary for the survival of animals and plants. Through this window, briefly opened onto a physically unattainable Dreaming, the soul gains access to the founding myths.

Contrasting a material, observable world with a spiritual one is not characteristic of pre-industrial, isolated communities. Over the centuries, individuals rebelling against their own times have fancied a past Golden Age. The expansion of capitalism triggered a violent, predictable reaction: modern society was blamed for caring only about action and profit, its literature was taxed with base realism and sordid materialism. But instead of looking backwards, writers and painters attempted to go beyond appearances and to discover at night the real universe we merely discern during sleep. Criticizing his epoch, the Age of Romanticism, Novalis wished for a future era when people 'would be simultaneously waking and asleep. Dreaming and at the same time not dreaming in a synthesis where both activities would strengthen each other.' From pre-Romanticism to Symbolism, intellectuals strove after a luminous nocturnal life likely to compensate for the narrowness of diurnal routines. Dreams became thus a means of access to the inexpressible. Coleridge, who called poetry 'a rationalized dream', saw dreams as the perfect degree of phantasy, and assumed that, while we are asleep, our sensations, and with them the emotions and passions they arouse, reaching their highest point, enable us to create wonderful pictures. Coleridge's 'ghost-world' was linked with a deep, internal universe, stronger than ordinary reality.

What was at stake was not merely a will to go beyond appearances, it was also the intellectuals' status in capitalist society. Before the eighteenth century, artists and writers conceived of themselves as pen- or pencil-workers. Their influence increased during the Age of Enlightenment, and they began to think they were different from other workers. What could substantiate such an idea? The fact that they had genius, and the capacity to listen to voices the majority could not hear – voices lacking external reality, perceptible only to the most gifted. Once 'our earthly cage has darkened' – once it is night and the others are asleep – 'our heart's genius tells us its harmonies', wrote Jean Paul (pseudonym of the German poet Johann Paul Richter). During sleep, Jean Paul assumed, living characters visit the poet, 'they whisper us their words'; the writer takes notice of their message and translates it into verses in the morning.

The value placed on dream activity was strengthened by the myth of the dreamed masterpiece. It is generally admitted that the solution of difficult problems can be found during sleep. Otto Loewi, the biologist who demonstrated how nervous impulses are transmitted through a chemical process, told how he had come to such conclusion by reasoning but was unable to demonstrate it until two dreams showed him the experiment likely to corroborate his hypothesis. He added that he had previously performed the same experiment in a different context: his dream had been nothing but the association of two antecedent ideas. Dreams may also be active in suggesting fresh, vivid scenes or new working procedures. The German painter Caspar David Friedrich borrowed from a dream the concentrated light that is characteristic of his oil paintings, and two episodes of *Dr Jekyll and Mr Hyde* were dreamed by Robert Louis Stevenson, who pointed out that the rest of the story had been written 'awake and consciously'.

The dreamed masterpiece is of a different nature: it is a revelation, something disclosed directly and in its entirety to the creator. Not surprisingly, the first, and one of the most famous cases, dates from the eighteenth century. When he was young, the Italian composer Tartini said in old age, he had fancied a pact with the Devil. The latter, still at night, had played a violin sonata and Tartini had reconstituted it after a fashion the following day. Another well-known example is Coleridge's composition of *Kubla Khan*, 'if that indeed can be called a composition in which all the images rose up before him as *things*', the poet commented; after awaking, 'taking his pen, ink and paper', he 'instantly and eagerly wrote down the lines that are presented' – only 30 lines because he was interrupted by 'a person from Porlock', and afterwards could not retrieve the other verses. There is no way of checking these anecdotes; what matters is the notion of an exceptional ability to transform odd, unexpected sensations into a literary work. 'Every man hath visions', Keats wrote in *The Fall of Hyperion*. But many, having not been 'well nurtured in their mother tongue', do not care about what they have seen at night. 'Poesy alone can tell her dreams'; the poet and the ordinary sleeper 'are distinct, diverse, sheer opposite, antipodes'. Subjected to superficial, short-lived impressions, the latter is unable to perceive the only important reality placed within people themselves, whereas the former, being an uncommonly gifted person, can explore such realms.

This sphere 'to which the familiar world is chaos', as Shelley said in *The Defence of Poetry*, is best penetrated during sleep. Therefore the poet must first free his mind from earthly preoccupations and then let it open to visions. Dream fostering was the dominant factor in such a programme. There was a strong contrast between those intellectuals who wanted and those who did not want to stimulate dreams, or at least to recall and transcribe them. Goethe, for instance, was very reserved about dreams: 'If only I could warn your wife and Mrs Stein [one of his best friends] against their interest in dreams . . . You become yourself a dream when you deal seriously with such phantoms', he wrote to the poet J. D. Herder. While dreams were central in many of his contemporaries' works, Goethe left few dream accounts, and dreams play little part in his books. In the second part of Goethe's *Faust*, Homunculus, the artificial creature, reports a vision, but it is a summary of Faust's longings and does not introduce the reader to any emotive or spiritual experience. From the *Roman de la rose* to *Alice's Adventures in Wonderland*, many fantastic, improbable stories turned out, at the end of the book or of the projection, to be a person's dream. The recourse to the false-dream stratagem is still helpful when making a film or novel more thrilling, or when multiplying the episodes and or accumulating surprises or dramatic reversals. But the late-eighteenth- and early nineteenth-century poets looked with scorn at the trite mechanism of a character falling asleep at the beginning of a fable and awakening at the end. This, in their view, was a pathetic trick. Theirs was an attempt to apprehend another, larger, underestimated universe, and to express it through poetry or graphic arts. By disturbing ordinary people's routines and opening new vistas for them, they turned themselves into bards of the invisible. As Chekhov said in *The Seagull*: 'We should show life neither as it is nor as it ought to be but as we see it in our dreams.'

Seeing, remembering, telling: there were intellectual circles, in the nineteenth century, whose members developed a thorough dream culture. The poet, Wagner says in *The Meistersingers of Nürnberg*, 'must note his dreams and interpret them'. Jean Paul boasted an ability to provoke and direct his dreams. Like most of his friends, he recorded and circulated his visions. Bettina Brentano's letters are filled with observations such as these: 'Yesterday, sleep's peace pervaded my soul. I woke from time to time, ideas occurred to me, I transcribed them with a pen, without expanding on them, without assessing their value'; or: 'Yesterday morning I fell asleep in my boat. I dreamed of music. What I wrote you yesterday evening, tired and half possessed, is a pale reflection of what was expressing itself inside me.' Many were probably tempted to embellish their recollections, Achid von Arnim warned his fiancée, Bettina: 'Record your dreams, but honestly, otherwise it's valueless, don't ornament them.' Phrasing fleeting visions necessarily implies distortions. But what matters for our study is not the accounts' unverifiable accuracy, it is rather the enthusiasm many writers expressed about dreams. Most of the time, probably when the dream had been set down immediately after awaking, the account seems less affected. Jean Paul again:

'18 March 1819. Dream: first the story of that night, long ago, in Leipzig, when, after a serious talk, I looked at my friend Oerthel, he looked at me and we were both frightened by our self. Then I said to Goethe, who was leaving: "After death, at least, we learn what our self is." He looked at me, his eyes filled with tears, and I was as frightened as in the past in Leipzig.'

The style of direct accounts reveals a personality. Let us compare the dreams Coleridge and Jean Paul had almost simultaneously, at the beginning of 1804. The former begins with an attempt to describe his state of mind: 'I dreamed among the wild melancholy things, all steeped in a deep dejection but not wholly unmingled with pleasure, that I came up into one of our Hospital wards.' The latter is immediately more factual: 'A dream where I glide, kiss women and say to Otto: "Tell me that I must awake and I'll awake."' Coleridge's human contacts are vague and disturbing, 'I was told' – by whom? – 'the image before my eyes was a wretched dwarf with only three fingers', the ghost of a former friend 'who in attempt to enlighten mankind had inflicted wounds on himself, and must hence forward live bed-ridden.' Jean Paul engages in an endless exchange with Otto: 'He did what I had asked him to do . . . I was lying in the same bed as him . . . He told me . . . I explained to him . . .'. However, always when dreaming, both poets react in a highly emotional way, and feel relieved when they awake. Coleridge: ' I burst at once into loud and vehement weeping, which at length, but after a considerable continuance, awakened me.' Jean Paul, still in a dream: 'I woke as distressed as after a nightmare', went on talking with Otto, 'finally came the real awakening'. For both, dreaming was an exciting, nerve-racking, enlightening experience.

Let us now fast forward a half-century to contrast Hebbel's and Ruskin's accounts. Precise and matter-of-fact, the former goes candidly to the core of 'a dream as beautiful as the sky but filled with horror', featuring a mirror that reflects a person's ageing process. The latter wavers between facts and impressions – 'dozed into the usual but not unpleasant dreams which I forgot but the end' – that is to say, the feeling of being somewhere without being able to say exactly where. Dreamtelling is a difficult, challenging exercise, and we shall explore it later. All I wish to stress here is the paramount importance of such activity for a long-lasting century: from Jean Paul to Kafka and Schnitzler, from Coleridge to Graham Greene and William Burroughs, five intellectual generations were intent on remembering and reporting their dreams.

All regarded their own or their friends' delusions as raw material useful for literary invention or philosophical investigation, and many considered dreaming an imaginative activity, an unconventional way of thinking by substituting pictures and sounds for words. Coleridge addressed Robert Southey about the mysterious, fascinating power of dreams. They accomplish, he wrote, 'a transmutation of the *succession* of *time* into the *juxtaposition* of *space,* by which the smallest impulses, if quickly and regularly recurrent, *aggregate* themselves.' Novalis was enthusiastic over the rapture brought by ethereal, unworldly visions perceived during sleep: 'The dream reveals us in a strange manner how easily our soul enters any object, turns instantly into this object.' Dreams, he insisted, would weaken readers' certainties by introducing moments of radical indeterminacy and change. The task for writers and artists was to create 'tales similar to dreams, not logically organized but based on associations like dreams'.

As Baudelaire said, 'there is something positively miraculous in sleep, this adventurous evening trip; a miracle whose mystery has been dulled by punctiliousness . . . Think rather of the *absurd, unpredictable dream* disconnected from the sleeper's character, life and passions! Such a dream – I shall call it hieroglyphic – features obviously *life's supernatural region.*' Reverse side, back, mirror's opposite face, were all then recurring expressions. Most nineteenth-century poets and painters tried neither to translate their delusions into limpid stories or well-ordered pictures nor to explain their significance. Wanting to help their public to pursue in daytime the exploration begun, but too quickly interrupted, at night they searched the words, shapes, rhymes, assonances and colours likely to bring into the mind the atmosphere and quality of flying nocturnal impressions.

Showing people what is beyond the curtain was considered a duty. What was to be found there? Beautiful, heavenly landscapes likely to help one to forget earth's wasted surface. Let us recall the widespread hostility towards industrialization and 'modernity'. In *Poetry and History* (1808) an apologia for the ancestral rustic way of life, Achim von Arnim, whose books were filled with ethereal, fairy-like visions, lamented the destruction resulting from land abandonment. If there was another kingdom than the one we know – and many believed in the existence of such a kingdom – dream-inspired poems were the best, maybe the only, clue about its existence the only way, as Arnim said, to 'bring back inside the eternal community a world which, because it is terrestrial, has lost touch with it'. What mattered was less the content than the language. Visionary texts must recourse to a florescence of coloured words, rare adjectives, amazing expressions in order to help reverie and desire flood forth. Nocturnal impressions were transcribed in metaphors of volcanoes, eruptions, rivers, grass, trees and torrents; the Milky Way poured throughout the sky, stars falling from heaven illuminated the scenery, the moon ascended 'passionately' bright, the morning shone gold-bright. Here are a few lines from Jean Paul's *The Invisible Lodge*:

> He went down into a meadow that stretched as far as the eye could see on beautiful planets touching each other. A rainbow made of suns lined like necklace pearls framed the sky. The

solar circle was sinking to set beyond the horizon, a brilliant mounted belt lay on the meadow's edge and these brilliants were thousands of purple suns.[8]

An enchantment. But also a disconcerting, impenetrable mystery, 'a boundless plain of sandy wilderness, all black and void', Wordsworth said. And Poe: 'Deserts, limitless, and of the most forlorn and awe inspiring character, spread themselves out before me. Immensely tall trunks of trees, gray and leafless, rose up in endless succession as far as the eye could reach.' Such evocations of distress and fear creeping over the sleeper were not atypical. Jean Paul, Coleridge and many others were alarmed by the darkness of night. 'I no longer knew who I was', the former wrote after an agonizing night, 'I had no more human thoughts . . . The world had vanished in an abyss, I was alone. Something dark and shapeless (I know neither what it was, nor whether it wasn't *myself appearing to me*) urged me to search the horizon.' In *The Pains of Sleep* Coleridge expressed the feeling of the transgression of human boundaries inspired by visions where his identity dissolved.[9] Delight and terror contradict each other, but the poets considered such contradiction characteristic of our nature. Echoing Jean Paul's self apparition in his vision – we have met twice such conviction in his accounts – a dreamed character tells the protagonist of E.T.A. Hoffmann's *The Devil's Elixir*: 'Your agony is inside you, it doesn't kill you because you live in it.' Hoffmann was especially sensitive to nocturnal life's inescapable ambiguity, and illustrated it repeatedly in his famous tales. During sleep his heroes, reaching another shore, are introduced to 'the world's soul' or to 'the spiritual principle of things'. Such a realm being too perfect for them to acclimatize to easily they are torn between acceptance and refusal. The theme of the double, of the poignant bewilderment experienced by the self confronting itself, haunts Hoffmann's dark fictions. There is no external obstacle:

Hoffmann's characters could contemplate the revelation they are offered at night, but their weakness makes them refuse to be enlightened. And such resistance is painful.

It is impossible to know whether the nineteenth-century poets were exceptionally nightmare prone, but nocturnal torments pervade their texts. Nerval's *Aurélia* calls up an agonizing succession of dreams, and the creatures dwelling in the narrator's mind are close to those evoked by Coleridge in the letter mentioned above. Lost in Daedalian corridors, the anonymous 'I' who reports his dreams was thunderstruck at a sinister spectacle. A giant figure coming level with the clouds, after gesticulating clumsily, fell in the middle of the courtyard, hitting its wings along the walls, and the narrator confesses: 'I could not help screaming in terror and this woke me up with a jump.' Ugly beasts, 'ghastly visions' (Wordsworth); a creature 'almost maddening me with fear' (Emily Brontë); 'evil spirits and dead bodies' (Southey); plagued horrible nights with 'horror, guilt and woe' (Coleridge).

Some, like Jean Paul or Coleridge, went through distressing hours of darkness, and Nerval transcribed what he remembered of torturing visions seen during a period of madness. But these men were writers. Though surprising and at times saddening, nocturnal life became their favourite source of inspiration. Its variety and unpredictability delighted them. Even Jean Paul, who did his best to monitor his dreams, admired their unforeseeable character. In the evening he focused his attention on a friend, hoping she would reappear at night; instead he was visited by unknown, fugitive but seducing figures. Dreaming was considered an inventive, constructive faculty, a special process likely to tease the sleeper by alternating delight and fear. Hoffmann's fantastic tales staged either delicious delusions or dreadful visions; his stories were arranged according to the dreams' emotional drive. The dream-life of poets was so rich and engrossing that they were tempted to mix up dreams and wakeful imagination; expanding on visions or inventing them was part of their ordinary intellectual life. Recast, amplified and embellished dreams served various purposes: they revealed the illusory nature of terrestrial existence and offered amazing glimpses of impalpable beauty.

Beyond Words

With *The Birth of Tragedy* Nietzsche propounded a synthesis of the three previous generations' beliefs about dreams. He celebrated the immediate apprehension of forms and figures provided by dreams and showed how such visions, severing ties with mundane appearances, allowed people to sense beneath the surface of daily routines some deeper reality likely to help them interpret life. But Nietzsche was specific in his praise; he also criticized the poets, who, instead of merely passing on a revelation to the others, wanted to embellish it, and evoked emphatically the wonders of a fanciful universe.

The Symbolists and Surrealists strengthened Nietzsche's severe comments. They had no difficulty in demonstrating how some dream narratives sound affected, pompous or naïve. Jean Paul's, for instance:

> '*I dreamed that, on a lovely May evening, I went for a walk. The stream was peacefully murmuring between the moonlit pebbles – a sweet zephyr was swinging the reeds – the good moon was beating down its light upon the sleeping hemisphere – God's creation was resting in solemn peace. Everything seemed to tempt us to heartfelt rest, which the hurly-burly of life doesn't give us.*'

With their glamorous, blossoming horizons and their bizarre, fading creatures, Jean Paul's accounts often read like fairy tales.[10] The early twentieth-century poets made it clear that in many cases the so-called mysterious sphere of dreams was merely what the writers produced by giving way to their fantasy. More important, they wondered if the notion of an invented dream attributed to a fabricated character was not an absurdity. Is not open-endedness the most surprising and gripping aspect of dreams? The dream state is a peculiar situation. The sleepers, not knowing whether what they feel and perceive is real or illusory, hesitate between abandon and reserve. A fictional text, when it tells of how the protagonist falls asleep and explains what she or he sees, bypasses the ambiguity of a dream. The reader is in no doubt: the alleged 'vision' is a learned word-picture, possibly fantastic but certainly not ambiguous.

The difficulty is not limited to written accounts. Although dreams are mostly visual, representing them on canvas or in drawings is almost as problematic as describing them, if the painter wants to make it clear that what is depicted is a person's internal, evanescent sensations. Due to the Bible and Christian hagiography's frequent reference to dreams, Western artists have often attempted to sketch God's nocturnal messages. Consider *Pharaoh's Dream* (overleaf), one of the three mosaics illustrating heavenly visions in the thirteenth-century Florence baptistery. The sovereign's closed eyes and leaning head suggest that he is asleep. His two dreams, the seven fat cows devoured by seven lean ones and the seven ripe ears swallowed by seven thin ones, are pictured on the mosaic's right sector. Genesis does not say anything about Pharaoh's position, but expands at length on the dream's content. The biblical narrative, with its episodes of destruction, is dramatic. In order to fill the frame the mosaicist has been obliged to contrive a series of details – the long upholstered seat, the patterned canopy – absent from the text. The two knights in medieval armour who are chatting on the left side have been added uniquely to counterpoise the right side's figures. The mosaic is a wonderful work of art, but its particulars – irrelevant for an understanding of the vision – catch our attention and make us miss the solemnity of the divine communication.

Other devices have been used to expound the image's oneiric character. For instance, in the case of the Wise Men's vision reported in St Matthew, the three men are lying in the same bed while an angel is giving them God's instructions; the first is fast asleep, the second's eyes are half-closed, the third is awake. Sometimes the sleeping person's hands are squeezed up against his eyelids in an effort of concentration. Or a thought bubble emanating from the head surrounds the revelation. In Renaissance and classical art the scheme was often extremely sophisticated. The character's shut eyes were oriented towards a space represented as a window, but deprived of depth and framed like a picture where an heavenly messenger was delivering some divine announcement. The tradition of 'naïve' dream depiction was perpetuated in the twentieth century by Marc Chagall. His is an interesting example. Sleepers on his canvas are unwinding; their relaxed bodies lend themselves to pleasant, peaceful fancies. His characters' visions, emphasized by a coloured halo, allude to legends or folk-tales; they are coherent stories and wittingly avoid the dream's lability and emotional unsteadiness.

Such works have been criticized not for their unquestionable artistic value but for their arguable reading of dreams. A forged vision, it has been argued, allows no room for imagination, while its inconsistency is what makes a dream delightful or worrying. Cesare Pavese attempted to elucidate the opposition between novels and dreams. During sleep, he argued, we are our vision's narrators, but, unlike the novelist, we ignore what will happen next; it is *our* tale but it is beyond our control.[11] Against the temptation of 'poeticizing' there has long been an effort to manifest dreams' basic inconclusiveness. We are not concerned here with the history of this endeavour, but with the way creative imagination was used to suggest such ambivalence.

What looks fascinating in these enterprises is their variety. All, in their own original way, give evidence of our dreams' elusive nature. Some emphasize the disparity between the sleepers, who are 'real' beings, and the flickering, half-blurred character of their impressions. Rembrandt's pen drawings of biblical sleepers contrast the men – he focused on Jacob, his son Joseph and St Joseph – and their visions (see over). The former are precisely delineated: a firm black border marks their head, chest and arms; they seem planted in the ground. On the other hand the latter are merely sketched: they are light silhouettes isolated in the sheet's white, empty part. Rembrandt does not report a vision, he hints at flitting appearances that crossed Jacob's or St Joseph's mind.

In the bottom left part of one design Rembrandt sketched an ill-defined form, maybe an object or a component of some unfinished scenery. Did not he allude to dreams' unstable background? German films in the 1920s usually labelled 'Expressionist' took advantage of such flimsiness. Using a faint or wavering lighting, sharp black and white oppositions, distorting mirrors, long streaks of fog . . . , they echoed the

transience of dreams. At times the scenery itself was changing, the things deprived of a definite place or shape were as imprecise and elusive as dreamed objects. Some pictures proceeded like nightmares. Pursued by indefinable adversaries, the protagonist had to flee through a fluctuating landscape without knowing where to go. For commercial purposes there was at the end of the films an explanation: the protagonist had been temporarily mad or a magician had made the characters hallucinate. However, these works were not all horror movies, the aim of some was not to please their spectators by frightening them but to offer a visual, imaginative equivalent of a sleeper's subjective perceptions.

Expressionist films confronted nocturnal and diurnal life. But is there always a clear-cut distinction between these states? Are there not circumstances where we fall asleep without being aware of it and adapt to our fancies as if we were still awake? Cinema, better than painting, can simulate such subtle transitions, as exemplified by several directors, notably Bergman and Luis Buñuel. In some of their movies, no sign informs the audience of the shift: characters and scenery remain identical. For a few minutes the viewers hesitate, not knowing whether what they are seeing is part of the story or is a side episode. A man in Buñuel's *The Discrete Charm of the Bourgeoisie* is carving a chicken that turns out to be a cardboard accessory. The man finds himself on a theatre stage; he does not know a single line of the play; he panics at the sight of an impatient audience and starts sweating. Was he already asleep when he sliced the fowl? Diurnal activities leave traces during sleep, and dream impressions affect our daytime. Are the two phases of sleeping and waking clearly marked? asked Buñuel. The protagonist of his *Tristana* visits a bell-tower. She is fascinated by the bell-clapper and tries in vain to set it in motion. Without any transition she sees her uncle and suitor's head forming the protruding part of the clapper, and she awakes from a nightmare. We did not see her falling asleep. Did the visit upset her, or was the visit the initial part of the dream?

By surprising their public, a few film-makers have attempted to display the most problematic aspects of our dreams. At night, individuals, surroundings, circumstances have no stability and time ceases to be a continuous flow: various epochs merge, we chat with long deceased people, or live again moments of our childhood. Movies are uniquely capable of rendering this. Caught between his newly married wife and a seductive young lady whose advances he would like to resist, Oliviero, main character of Buñuel's *Mexican Bus Ride*, betrays his anxiety and desires during sleep. What is original is not the hackneyed love triangle but the cinematic treatment of Oliveiro's visions, where religious prohibitions, parental warnings, literary influences and sexual attraction combine uneasily. Biting into an apple, the woman offers Oliveiro a piece that becomes a long thread leading to the young man's mother mounted on a pedestal. Or she approaches in a bathing suit, but the wife suddenly rises out of the water. Oliveiro wants to throw the woman into the river, but it is his wife who falls in. He wants to kiss her, but finds the other under his lips. Fleeting images shot against a blurred background associate recent and ancient events, old fears and distressing substitutions. The young man does not comment on his fantasies; spectators can read a violent struggle against temptation or the wishful fulfilment of repressed lust.

For the Surrealists,[12] films were unable to match the fickleness of dreams, they but could represent our mind's dreaming state. Buñuel was involved in Surrealism: his first films, *The Golden Age* and *The Andalusian Dog*, were meant to illustrate a dream's idiosyncratic development without reference to any sleeping individual. Who was dreaming, a woman or a man? Young or elderly were irrelevant queries; these were anonymous fantasies with obvious sexual hints, a touch of sadism, formal associations and recurring images redirecting or modifying the delusion. Despite some enthusiastic approval, the films did not reach a vast public and Buñuel, while refusing to interpret the visions attributed to Oliviero, Tristana or other characters, inserted them into a continuous, comprehensible story. In doing so he gave up his Surrealist creed.

Surrealism was short-lived. Rarely did a small group of writers and artists, coming together for a few years and then dispersing, enjoy so much prestige. The Surrealists were very close, had frequent meetings, organized happenings, supported each other. Initially their aim was to free human imagination from the burden of civic, social and family duties. They celebrated our mind's mobility and inventiveness, urged their contemporaries to enter the realm of the unimagined, the reversible, the indeterminate. They let their pens race automatically across the paper in a trance: images came unconsciously and assembled in a poem. Then they turned to dreams. What linked them for a time and made them different was their dedication to the creation and diffusion of dreams.

We have encountered numerous examples of societies or individual profoundly concerned with dreams. The Surrealists were comparable to none. For the great majority dreams were a window onto another world. Some conceived of this realm as existing somewhere and being able to influence humanity. Others thought it belonged to a remote past. And still others wanted to recreate it, thanks to poetry. On the other hand, for the Surrealists our sleeping life was not something distinct and mysterious, it was an integral part of our self, a part as important as our waking activities. Business, profit and economic concerns have made us reduce night to a mere compensation for our daily efforts; we are no longer capable of letting our sleeping self wander and use our mind's powerful expressive force to create prodigious images and whimsical tales in a concert of multiple voices. If we go on equating sleep and rest, our nights will be dead periods and death will slowly overcome us. There is no way to keep in good health and survive except by letting our nocturnal fantasies blossom. The Surrealists had faith in a revolution not because they were sorry for the poor and the exploited, but because a radical change was the best way of restoring our dreaming capacity.

There was something naïve in such infatuation for dreams. Surrealism, not being a school as such, was receptive to the ideas and fashions flourishing in Europe between the World Wars. It borrowed from Marxism in its attacks against alienation in capitalism. Its marvelling at the 'elasticity' of dreamed time – its tendency to run fast or to be slow or even to be never-ending – was inspired by a quick reading of papers on relativity. There was also a call on Freud's services. However, while drawing from various sources, the Surrealists were able to maintain their own, original line. Take the case of Freudianism. Freud was much concerned about dreams, but, in his view, they expressed something hidden, and once translated would give access to something else – the unconscious. He considered them essential no more and no less than any other outward sign of concealed wishes, such as puns or slips of the tongue. The Surrealists rejected the opposition conscious/unconscious and every other dichotomy, such as real versus illusory or reason versus imagination. For them dreams were not the manifest but the distorted aspect of a concealed desire; they were one of the human species' fundamental aspects. More precisely, they were desire itself in its most radical form. People, they contended, are driven by their wants. They do their best to survive, to find love, health and happiness. These are all clear needs, usually deriving from our place in society. Above them exists a pure desire, dense, unfathomable, inexpressible in words. This is what dreams arouse when they are not repressed.

Answering an opinion poll about dreams in 1925, René Crevel, one of the Surrealists, explained what dreams meant for him and his friends:

> I dream without words or images. Rather: the dreams that influenced me and even sometimes determined my conscious

life were deprived of words and images. A state of mind silently overcomes my soul at night. And then comes, when I wake, the authoritative remembrance of an intense excitement. The precise object that motivated it is of no importance.[13]

A dream may be a sensation, a scream, a colour, a brief and violent image. Michel Leiris's dream collection is possibly the most typical gathering of nocturnal perceptions written out immediately, without any attempt to recall all the details: 'A three branch tree (they are snakes) is knocking on my window pane wearing a ready-made suit and a wing collar.'[14]

Visual representations, drawings, collages, cut-outs, ideograms, sketches and photographs were considered particularly apt to render the impressive power of dreams, provided they did not tell a story but went straight into the mind's eye by transcribing an effect produced on the sleeper. There were thus infinite landscapes with day-as-night skies, long, overwhelming shadows or penetrating light rays, giant eyeballs, windows indefinitely opening onto other windows, threatening half-human, half-mechanical structures or, in Miro's paintings and Giacometti's sculptures, shapes aimed to strike and stir the onlooker without representing anything identifiable. Any attempt to communicate a vision was meant not only to allow the dreamers to externalize their yearning but also to give their readers or spectators access to the fundamental human investments of desire.

The Surrealists disagreed on many issues, namely politics, literature, love and sexuality, but their investment in the mind's dreaming activities helped their group to survive for about a decade. After their estrangement, most continued to care about their personal dreams. Let us leave aside their peculiar hypothesis about day/night complementarity. These were young men keen to remember what they had fantasized about during sleep, and in that way they were little different from those we encountered earlier in this chapter. Medical research has proved – it is one of its few undisputed conclusions – that all of us have dreams. Some do not remember, but laboratory experimentation has also shown how remembering is to a large extent intentional. Individuals who are convinced they never dream begin to recall impressions or images as soon as their attention has been attracted to the phenomenon. Michel Leiris entitled his dream collection *Nights Without Night*. Trained people, he assumed, prepare their dreams (think of Jean Paul conjuring in the evening the women he would have liked to meet at night); they are half-conscious during sleep and summon up easily their dreams by day. So their nights filled with fantasies ignore the black, empty night.

If small intellectual circles were able to stimulate dreams and make them the centre of their poetic creation, we can guess what part dreams played, and still play, in isolated, pre-industrial societies. Wondering about the meaning and potential reality of one's own visions, communicating them, asking for advice, creates strong links between a community's members. We have noted how a 'Europeanized' Cambodian readjusts to a fleeting spirits' world when he returns home because, otherwise, he would be an alien. Collective dreamtelling has an aggregative power, it allows relators and listeners – that is to say, everybody – to share a joint experience. There are hierarchies, as in most human relationships: the shaman has visions more complicated and authoritative than anyone else, and dream interpreters are regarded as authorities by their fellows. Differences arise even among writers, Achid von Arnim or Charles Lamb contrasted the wealth of Jean Paul's or Coleridge's fancies with the dryness of their own. Dream-based associations, like most social formations, undergo tensions and conflicts, but those are transposed from the material sphere to that of the imagination. The magic of dreams is their remoteness from ordinary life. It is also what makes them puzzling. Even those spellbound in dreams cannot help but ask: what are they made of and where do they come from?

CHAPTER TWO

Who can tell us what Dreams are?

Do dreams allow our brains to restore themselves? Or do they help us to solve intricate problems? Are they warnings that prepare us for future events, wish fulfilments or fantasies? Although dreams resist our attempts to account for them, people have always been eager to penetrate their apparent secrets. The same, very simple but ever unsettled questions have long been preoccupying thinkers as well as the man or woman in the street: How are dreams formed? What do they mean?

Dream theories all deal with the same material – dreams reported by sleepers after they awake. These dreams reappear in and through the ways people survey them, talk about them, sift them. Yet, far from attempting to interpret the few uncontroversial aspects of dreams, commentators prefer to disagree, putting forward contradictory explanations. If they choose to develop unprovable assumptions rather than scrutinize our limited knowledge of dreams, we may, not unreasonably, ask ourselves what their aim is. I would like to show how most dream theories have as their real subject not our dreams but a few fundamental problems regarding the significance of human existence. The queries raised about dreams are in fact related to other topics, such as personality characteristics, the possible existence of extra-human entities, the potential relationship of these entities with humans, or, more simply, our instincts and needs, such as sex, love or loathing. If different ways of explaining the origin of dreams are incommensurable, all are quite related to a continual questioning about human destiny. It is against this background that the present chapter should be read.

A Mere Fading of Consciousness?

The very category of the 'dream-state' is a controversial one. There have long been serious arguments about the respective status of waking and sleeping, some thinkers assuming that the fading of consciousness is merely a different phase of human life, others believing there were two radically distinct states, and that dreams, being independent of conscious will, are close to madness. Plato offers a good example of a shrewd mind in a quandary about the nature of dreams. In the *Timaeus* he states successively that when our bodies are quiet we enjoy an almost dreamless sleep (§ 45) and that, in the same conditions, the soul is absorbed in divinatory dreams (§ 71). It is tempting to laugh at Plato's difficulty, but the concepts we use today are not straightforward and, like Plato's 'quiet' sleep, adapt easily to conflicting interpretations.

The debate is not new. Both Plato and Aristotle tackled the enigma and resolved it in fairly inconsistent ways. We consider them the founding fathers of both Western and Arabic philosophy, but they were also heirs to an antecedent, now forgotten, tradition of theoretical reflection. Their answers to the dream quandary mirror what was said before them and attest to a longlasting anxiety about dreams. What is at stake here is the essence of the human self. Are we unified or split? Is there in the being that is our self something unknown, an internal impetus we ignore? Since they elude our conscious will, dreams are central in the debate about the potential dual structure of human beings. If we are divided, we are a combination of different entities, all part of our selves that, together, make what we are but to a certain extent overlook or even contradict each other.

Against the dualist point of view, a few physiologists, for example the Austrian Frederick Perls, maintain that dreams are mere translations of body sensations. While acknowledging the fact that dream periods are characterised by REM and a low level of muscular activity, these scientists[1] insist that no correlation has ever been established between the sleeping body's condition and the content of dreams: all sleepers react in the same way, but their dreams are radically different. It cannot even be proved that eye movements signal visual experiences. It is therefore wiser and more consonant with the present state of our knowledge to assume that the stimulation of parts of our person by external events or by internal perceptions provokes synaesthetic reactions that, being mechanical, cannot mean anything. Only afterwards when we attempt to remember, do we credit them with an intelligible content likely to be capable of interpretation. Waking and sleeping are two different states of a unique being. Judging from the ancient literature available to us today, Aristotle was the first to develop systematically such a theory. Concerned as he was with dreaming he wrote three short essays on the topic.[2] How, Aristotle asked, can we characterize superior beings? By the fact that they *perceive*, in other words that they are aware of some aspects of the physical world: 'waking consists in nothing else than the exercise of perception through senses'. While small organisms whose only task is survival require no rest, superior beings who must be alert to surrounding signals cannot always be vigilant and have to relax. Sleep is the obverse of our active life. Wakefulness is the free play of our faculties; sleep limits the same faculties.

What is crucial in Aristotle's scheme is that sleep affects our sensory capacity, since the impressions present in dreams are exactly those manifest by day. But in the waking state our minds are monitored by perception and understanding, while in sleep we do not perceive. If we wish to apprehend the origin of dreams we must start from the waking state: perception creates sensations; many things are present to our senses, and we select those we deem important; yet impressions not singled out can leave a trace. Dreams result from excitement, whether generated by the outer world or from within our body during the day. However, in the waking state, such disturbances are controlled by our intellects. In slumber they are carried to the centre of sensation, where they display themselves. Different images no longer under the guidance of an intellect are liberated and actualize in accordance with the movements of the sensory organs or the impulses stemming from the outer world. Dreams are visual and aural presentations caused by our sense impressions under inhibited judgement.

Aristotle's views on dreams are fundamental. It is often argued that, before the seventeenth century, dreams were seen as signs sent by mysterious forces alien to the material world. In the fourth century BC, Aristotle was already insisting that dreams were self-generated. He attempted to explain the two states of waking and sleep in reference to blood circulation. His was a scientific demonstration, even if his understanding of the way the heart functioned is far removed from contemporary knowledge. Not content with developing a technical argument Aristotle appealed to the reader's common sense: 'What I emphasize here is true . . . , everybody can be convinced by paying attention and trying to remember the impressions we feel when we sink into sleep or when we are awake. When just about to waken one will sometimes catch the images which form in sleep and find that they are nothing but movements lying in the organs of sense.'[3]

Doctrines that conceive of humans and their actions as governed and given meaning by awareness and intuition do not consider sleep a specific state, one totally different from the waking state. Descartes used the dreaming/waking pairing to strengthen his theory of a united human consciousness. Humans, in his system, were a combination of flesh and spirit. The body was the weaker of the two, obliged to indulge in periods of rest, while the mind was active even in slumber. In dreams, Descartes contended, we see, hear, judge, decide; our brains do not stop functioning, we are only hampered by the passivity of our limbs, unable to respond to the brain. We may sometimes doubt whether diurnal life is not an illusion and that the 'real' world is not the world of our dreams. There is no way of deciding. Yet this hardly matters, since our spirit is equally active in both states. In other words, the human soul is always conscious in any circumstances. As Descartes wrote in the fourth part of his *Discourse on Method*, 'all the same thoughts and conceptions that we have while awake may also come to us in sleep', so that that everything we distinguish clearly is true, even if we are dreaming.

Rationalism in its various aspects derived from Cartesianism dominated European thought until the twentieth century. Philosophers and scientists took it for granted that, thanks to introspection, human beings could train to become aware of their diurnal or nocturnal emotions. I noted earlier that, in the 1950s, doctors were collecting extensive series of observations about their own dreams and the dreams of their colleagues and students. What is of interest here are the psychological mechanisms that were at work in their investigations. Starting with the idea that any impression has a rational explanation, scientists sought to disentangle the elements of the chain and to link the dream images to objective, discernible factors. It occurred to them that dreams consist of the unfolding of reminiscences and of the superimposition of related images. This meant that encounters made by day or drawings or pictures seen previously were reused during night. Until then there was nothing new with respect to Aristotle; only the vocabulary had changed and sounded more 'modern'. Using serious observations, academics contended that diurnal images were stored in the memory, forgotten, and then later modified by the imagination. But they had to account for the presence of blurred, imprecise images and to explain how these images combined. The answer was found in a contemporary invention, highly fashionable in the 1850s and 1860s, namely photography. A snapshot is often fuzzy. In the same way something we have seen by the way will result in a fuzzy mental image. The combination of images resembles a superimposition of several pictures. Dreams were interpreted as optical groupings of images that had something in common or were related to the same topic.

Gérard Grandville (1803–47), a French artist passionately interested in dreams, perfectly illustrated this associationist theory, according to which every visual detail, however bizarre, is based on something the sleeper has seen in waking life. A man dreams he has committed a murder. Death evokes a cross. The cross resembles a pair of scales. That gives the idea of Justice and brings forth Justice's eye. Wanting to escape, the sleeper mounts a horse but falls into the sea, where he would be devoured by a shark were it not for a cross.

If we were content with taking an overall picture of dream interpretations we might come to the conclusion that the initially impressionistic descriptions made by nineteenth-century clinicians developed by stages into a more precise knowledge based on strict procedures. But what I am trying to show is that dream theories, far from unfolding harmoniously, followed the evolution of scientific investigation and reflected the contemporary philosophical trend. Dream accounts gathered in the nineteenth century are still valid because of their accuracy and precision. Moreover, they inform us about the patterns of dream reporting in force at the time. On the other hand, the theories based on that material tell us more about the philosophical or physiological conceptions of the period than about the very nature of dreams. The following pages will corroborate this statement.

Dreams, or the Enemy Within

We could stress the fact that introspection, conceived by Descartes, was rather naïve, but this would initiate a useless debate, since there is a much more simple difficulty with the idea of an unified self. St Augustine had pointed out the quandary in his *Confessions*. Drawing on Augustine to make a stand against Descartes may seem anachronistic. However, this is not a book of history but an anthropological study dealing with human, basic, recurring attitudes concerning the mystery of dreams. In this respect the all-important is not the chronology but the relevance of the arguments.

The young Augustine lived a dissolute life and spent his money carelessly. He later converted to Christianity and gave up what he considered the errors of youth. But he could not help dreaming. He was much upset by this, since he experienced in his dreams the carnal pleasures he now condemned. He wondered whether, when asleep, he was truly himself: 'Where is then my reason which, when I am awake, helps my mind to resist temptation? Does my reason shut together with my eyes?' On awakening he became aware of what had happened in his dreams and felt ashamed. Was it his conscious self that not only had indulged in forbidden acts but enjoyed them too? Was he not allowed to postulate a difference between the waking self and the sleeping one?[4]

Augustine was a rational thinker whose notion of dreams was, as we shall see, extremely careful and did not comply with popular superstitions tolerated by other bishops. And yet, in *The City of God*,[5] he ventured to suggest a distinction between a man's body and his 'phantom'; he felt uneasy about the idea, but was impressed by the variety of objects seen in dreams. Was it not possible, in exceptional circumstances, with the help of some drug, for the 'ghost' of a dreamer to receive 'shapes that are like material bodies' and wander during a few days across the world?

St Augustine's remorseful hesitations must be taken seriously, for they remind us that splitting human beings into two different parts and contrasting their good and bad sides would solve many problems, first and foremost the question of dreaming. The eclipse of the notions of space and time, such as they are experienced in waking life, the impossibility of stopping dream images and reordering them have always impressed observers. In the Bible, what looks elusive is compared to a dream: 'He shall fly away as a dream' (Job, 20, 8). Such an uneasy feeling was echoed both by Homer and Euripides. In the *Odyssey* (XIX, 560), Penelope advises Odysseus, whom she has not yet recognized: 'My guest, I know how vain dreams are and how obscure is their language. I know that, for human beings, few of them come true.' In *Iphigeneia Among the Taurians* (c. 415 BC), Euripides warns us that 'Not even gods whom men call wise are less deceptive than the flying dreams' (lines 571–2).

Since dreams seem deceptive and baffle our vigilance, why do we not suppose that sleep is something specific, a state radically different from waking, in which the division of the personality reaches its zenith? Plato was adamant on that point: three long passages of *The Republic*[6] stressed the obscure, dark, uncivilized and uncomfortable nature of dreams. 'Is not the dream state just this: the mistaking of a semblance for the reality it resembles?' Plato was not content with describing dreams as perfectly subjective states of mind that were of little importance compared with physical reality. Many opinions on dreams are, in fact, statements about the general meaning of life. Such was the case with the Greek philosopher. Human beings, Plato contended, are surrounded by temptations, but in so far as they are decent people they resist them. The most vulgar passions 'are awakened in sleep when the other part of the soul, the rational, refined and dominant part, slumbers'. In this awkward situation

the bestial and savage part allows itself total freedom and, gaining control of sleep, makes its best to rush out and satisfy its own instincts. There is nothing it will not make to free itself from all sense of shame and reason. It does not hesitate to fancy going to bed with a mother or anyone else, man, god or animal. It is ready for any bloody action. It does not abstain from any food. In short, it avoids no excess of insanity or degradation.

Plato did not exemplify his attacks, but incestuous fancies were not rare in the Greek literature of his time. For instance, Herodotus, relating how an ambitious Athenian politician dreamed of sleeping with his mother, did not blame the dream but mocked the man who interpreted it to signify that he would rule the city.[7]

Such cynicism made Plato indignant. This, he assumed, proved the double nature of human beings. Our bestial drives induce us to enjoy pleasures that our conscious self is unaware of, but that are indirectly expressed among other things in dreams. Plato aimed at moralizing Greek cities; his view of dreams helped him to distinguish the luminous and the sinister sides of human nature. His cure for blameable dreams went in the same direction: he urged people to rouse the rational side of their minds before going to sleep. In doing so they would sleep quietly and their best part would not be disturbed by pleasure or discomfort. Moreover, they would be able to apprehend things they did not know hitherto. If a man has 'tamed the passionate part in his soul and activated the part in which reason resides, he is most likely to apprehend truth'.

Plato's contrasted, black and white point of view was not exceptional in his time; other thinkers admitted that the self was not unified but dissociated into the two parts that form human personality. What was unusual with Plato was his introduction of dreams into the picture. He could have chosen many examples to illustrate the blend of the dutiful and corrupt in human nature, for instance the case of murderers who are ideal fathers and faithful friends, but he singled out dreams to prove that the enemy is within.

Plato's intellectual atmosphere has to be taken into account: dream interpretation is always concerned with the role that such exegeses play in social life. It would be misleading to speak of a Greek conception of dreams, for contradictory opinions were expressed simultaneously, and often by the same people. But it seems that there was then a pessimistic understanding of dreaming. In the *Iliad* (II, 6), the (personified) dream sent by Zeus to Agamemnon was labelled, by the poet and then by Zeus himself, as 'harmful'. For Euripides, who wrote it twice, in *Hecuba* and in *Iphigeneia Among the Taurians*, the 'black-winged' dreams were born out of Mother Earth's dark womb.[8] In the *Odyssey* (XXIV, 11–12) 'the country of dreams' was located next to the Underworld, where the shadows of the dead lead a miserable existence. A few texts describe the sleeper's soul leaving the body and going to this realm of the dead in order to dream, and a trace of this negative judgment (which, I insist, was not universally accepted) is to be found in Ovid's *Metamorphoses* (XI, 592ff.), where Juno sends Iris to the palace of the god Slumber, a gloomy, dark cave inhabited by the 'deceitful dreams' stored there, 'as numerous as leaves in the woods', waiting for visitors to pick them up.

Yet a reference to the historical context is insufficient. The bright posterity of Plato's speculation shows that much more than the spirit of the epoch was at stake. Plutarch, who made important comments on the topic, used dreams to distinguish social categories.[9] Dreams, food and sex were the few physical experiences common to all classes, and it is not by chance that Plato denounced the dreams that involved food or copulation. Dreams, Plutarch glossed, reveal the quality of the human soul. Ordinary individuals hope they will find inspiration in a deity when they are asleep, and those with the foulest minds satisfy their worst desires. On the other hand, those who resist and master their bad impulses deserve divine inspiration; their dreams are clean, and the growing decency of their dreams is the measure of their virtue. Like Plato, Plutarch stressed the double nature of humanity: a combination of high aspirations and bad instincts. Like his predecessor, Plutarch maintained that all souls are not equal: the best spirits, *oi aristoi*, the aristocrats, master their impulses; their rational soul allows them to have only beautiful, pure nocturnal images.

Plato's *Republic* was a utopia, the picture of an ideal, elitist society where the rightness of dreams and thoughts would be a discriminant, a characteristic likely to distinguish the best citizens from the others. Both Plato and Plutarch elaborated what was a widespread conviction. After them Synesius of Cyrene, a landowner and a high ecclesiastical dignitary, a typical member of the Roman nobility, assumed that imaginative minds like his own were able to determine the direction of their nocturnal visions and understand the highest things that, of course, were out of the herd's reach. The belief that superior minds are capable of rare dreams has never vanished. Thomas Browne, a seventeenth-century English physician, urged his friends to indulge during the day in virtuous thoughts which would 'lay up good treasures for the night, whereby the impressions of imaginary forms arise into sober similitudes preparatory unto divine impressions'.[10] 'The dreamer must be stronger than his dream', Victor Hugo trumpeted, while Graham Greene claimed that in slumber he left 'the common world' to retreat to an inner 'world of his own', where he lived a purely individual, hidden life.[11]

We forget parts of our dreams, and only through our descriptions do others know anything of them. Is it not possible to suppose that in past periods, in Plato's view, 'the noblest minds' learned to censure their smutty fantasies and always gave a clean account of their dreams? Aristocrats should repress their 'bestial and savage part' in three fields – sex, crime and food, but the former received the longest exposition in the *Republic*. This brings us back to Augustine's worries, and in this wake to Christian speculations on dreams. There is no Christian doctrine on the matter; various, often contradictory, opinions have been expressed about them. However, dreams were soon a puzzle for the Church Fathers and their followers. Why were the very pious, the most faithful, thinking at night of exquisite meals and erotic pleasures? Augustine's suggestions regarding the double nature of human beings could not meet the required purpose, since it was impossible to admit that God had made his favourite creation half-good, half-bad. As we shall see, an external agent, the Devil, helped to solve the matter. However, according to Christian doctrine, Satan was unable to impose his authority on true believers. All he could do was to induce them to sin by showing tempting images. It was essential, therefore, to prepare for a blessed night, since, depending on the state of the dreamer's soul, the images seen in dreams could represent the most sinful illusions or the highest truths. Although they based their opinions on different grounds, Plato and some Christian thinkers arrived at the same conclusion: the best people were capable of purified dreams. Freud had this in mind when he stated that the images capable of making their way into a dream were only those accepted by the censorship.[12] Exercise your mind and it will repel dirty pictures. 'On Dreams', a short article Freud published a year after *The Interpretation of Dreams* appeared, explained how his method dealt 'with the mechanism of the dream-work as well as with the nature and conditions of what is described as repression'.[13]

There are situations, dream walking for instance, where people act without knowing what they are doing. There is a purpose in their enterprise, but they are not conscious of this aim. The only way to make sense of their behaviour, Freud suggested, is to postulate the presence in ourselves of an obscure area, the unconscious, whose existence is proved indirectly by movements unintended by consciousness. In the last decades of the twentieth century, it became fashionable to make an inventory of Freud's weaknesses.[14] It was then emphasized that, far from being new, his notion of the unconscious had surfaced at least 30 years before *The Interpretation of Dreams* and had been immediately accepted. Freud did no more than schematize it, forgetting that there are various levels of consciousness, and that the sleeper remains mentally alert.

Undoubtedly the adjective and noun 'unconscious' had often been used during the nineteenth century, but their meanings were then imprecise. They referred to vitality or instinct, to what we do automatically, to what was felt but could not be phrased. Wordsworth, in *The Prelude*, stated that he held 'unconscious intercourse with beauty'; the Swiss philosopher Henri Frédéric Amiel (1821–81) noted in his diary that his 'unconscious life' fed his imagination. Freud borrowed the term but reworked it entirely; he theorized the unconscious as the initial part of the self, present at birth, before socialization by external influences that would develop our consciousness, without ever destroying the obscure side of our psychic apparatus.

Freud's dynamic vision did not confine itself with fancying a moral conflict between good and bad impulses in human souls, so that putting here side by side his sophisticated, knowledgeable investigations and Plato's abrupt statements may seem odd. Again, we do not ponder the scientific merit of dream theories but probe their ideological groundwork. Freud pictured a divided self caught between primitive instinct and civilized, conscious choice. Let us consider his description of the unconscious: it is 'the dark, inaccessible part of our personality'; the little we know of it 'is of a negative character' and is the reverse of the conscious. 'We call it a chaos . . . filled with energy reaching it from the instincts.' Deprived of structure or organization it tends exclusively 'to bring about the satisfaction of instinctive needs subject to the observance of the pleasure principle'.[15] This impressive, almost apocalyptic, passage reminds us of texts in which we found, earlier, a ferocious portrayal of one corrupt human face. If the intellectual framework is different, the conclusion is identical: the enemy is within.

According to Freud, dreams are the royal road to a knowledge of the unconscious. The brutal part of ourselves, the internal foe, has desires whose fulfilment is prohibited by society, for instance the wish to have sex with one's parents. Such lascivious appetites surface by night when the conscious is asleep. They are so adverse to accepted conventions that dreamers would awake horrified if repression did not translate unwelcome images into acceptable ones. In order to protect a slumber necessary to the body's survival, unacceptable ideas must not appear in dreams but 'be replaced by hints, allusions' or indirect representations that 'must not be immediately intelligible' so that what is then remembered, the manifest content, is a disguise of a latent content that psychoanalysis will try to disclose.

Many objections have long been raised against Freud. He maintained that dreams are based on wish fulfilment, which is not always true (this Freud later admitted). He thought that we forget dreams because of their dangerous implications, whereas we often remember and even interpret them. He wrongly likened dreams to abnormal psychic phenomena and failed to understand that they are a necessary part of sleep. I am unable to appraise the relevance of Freud's system, nor is it the purpose of this book; I merely wish to understand the philosophical presuppositions that form the basis of his system by drawing attention to its historical and sociological background and to the form of life in which it was embedded.

The potential relationship between dream and madness had been repeatedly explored in the eighteenth and nineteenth centuries and had become a permanent, almost obsessive concern for some observers. Coleridge was much impressed by the case of his friend Charles Lloyd: 'all realities round him mingle with and form a part of his strange dream'; his mind, perceiving impressions from without, transforms them into images; these fancies take the place of an external reality, but seem as vivid as actual sensations. Gérard de Nerval, in his autobiographical novel *Aurélia* (1855), linked mental illness with 'the encroachment of dream upon real life'; he showed how the overflow of dreams into waking life could result in a split personality, an idea corroborated by contemporary physiologists, who believed that in various instances the human mind could be fragmented. Thus, when Freud considered a dream a nocturnal psychosis caused by a motor paralysis, he confirmed what was already relatively clear. But he was not content with noting that the sleeper relinquishes all perception of the physical world and with labelling dreams as an already somewhat disturbed form of mental activity. He offered an interpretation and opened the way to a cure by presenting the dream as a laborious compromise between the unconscious and repression. In his view the sleeper was not simply overwhelmed by maddening, nonsensical images: all these fantasies had meaning, meaning that psychoanalysis could exploit to reveal the original trauma that had provoked psychic instability.

This is but one example of Freud's close relationship with the medical concerns of his time and the way he transcended them by presenting a far-reaching, coherent, well-researched system. Today Freud has been neither forgotten nor surpassed; his method of close textual analysis has simply been replaced by data computerization. The wonder is that, despite the advent of more elaborated practices, *The Interpretation of Dreams* is still widely read. A glance taken at the conflicting theories developed at present is likely to explain this paradox. Contemporary researchers disagree on the origin of dreams. Some contend that the cortex, which monitors our reactions to the outer world, falters at night and tolerates fantasies that it will cancel when alert. Others stress the reactions provoked by the autonomic nervous system, which, being purely visceral, cannot be recalled. Technically, doctors or scientists may be right, but their views are colourless, ignore the fantastic variety of dreams and give the impression that no theory of them is easily available.

Freud's hypothesis was based on a process, it was not limited to a series of figures or to neural activity located in some sector of the brain. When we are unable to link together various phenomena that none the less seem related to one another, a good solution is often to hypothesize their common factor. The postulate may turn out to be wrong but for a while it can help to systematize the investigations. This Freud did wonderfully when he contrived an elegant solution for a long-lasting enigma. His was the last system based on a conflict between good and evil, between civilization and the jungle. Such antagonism could not but appeal to readers who had long been (and are still) enthralled by elementary confrontations in novels, comic strips, films and television programmes. *The Interpretation of Dreams* is a twentieth-century literary masterpiece. Well-written, easy to understand, filled with enticing dream accounts, it meets both the demand for scholarly explanation and the longing for good stories that characterize people who enjoyed secondary schooling, namely the majority who live in industrialized countries. Faced with aspects of their experience that do not materialize and are therefore apprehended intuitively, humans forge concepts and allow them to delimit and name what cannot be observed. The notion that any of us are inhabited by an unconscious that can be explored thanks to an exegesis of our dreams was a ingenious construct, and – many argue – one that still stands after more than a century. Our thinking has been fundamentally marked by Freud's theories; they permeate everyday culture and have attracted many disciples from the humanities and social sciences.

'Born on the actual efflux of my will I flie'

Analyses of dreams explored up to now seem torn between two opposed accounts that stress respectively the unity of the self and its division between a clear, conscious part and a dark, unconscious one. According to the former interpretation, our logical organizing system is weakened in sleep by a disruptive tendency; dreams do not express anything, or express very little, but they may be important because of the debates they cause. The latter theories contend that, by night, the hidden side of our personality tries to manifest itself, but they disagree on the issue of the conflict. It would be meaningless to look for a synthesis of these schemes, since they are far from exhausting the debate. Other systems opt for a complete separation between two independent principles, individuals being, in their view, made of a spiritual 'inward self' and a material body.

In one of his *Philosophical Poems*, 'Insomnium Philosophicum', the English poet and philosopher Henry More (1614–87), fancied that while his sleeping body was lying down, as dead as a corpse, himself, his very *I*, 'born on the actual efflux' of his will, was flying 'more swift than thought, in endless spaces'. Henry More, we may venture, did not believe that form and substance, body and spirit could separate, but his refined poem was the mere renewal of an old assumption, according to which in sleep the soul, liberated from the body and freed from worldly concerns, has access to superior realities. The tradition was still very much alive in the seventeenth century, since Milton, however sceptical he was regarding the mystical origin of dreams, did not hesitate to evoke in his *Fifth Elegy* the wandering of his mind 'quit of the body' in sleep.

Should we regard all these fantasies about the temporary partition of human beings as inconsequential fancies? If so, we would misunderstand what such accounts were really all about. They served in the past, and may still serve, although in a more sophisticated manner, to use dreaming as a tool likely to elucidate the functioning of the human mind. In the Hindi tradition mentioned earlier, matters have been carried to extremes to the extent that human constituents, flesh and soul, are in conflict with each other. In this instance, dream and reality become ambiguous. Since people believe that, by trying to control themselves, they can take their souls out of their bodies, move from one universe to another and in some mysterious way visit the places and people they see in a dream, the boundaries between slumber and wakefulness tend to be reversed. What happens daily is considered a mere illusion, and the very notion of dreams, as conceived in Western thought, becomes useless.

Without going that far, other beliefs affirm that our spirit, locked up in the flesh, surrounded by worldly cares, is unable to open to truth except in sleep when, withdrawn from contact with matter, it comprehends the world. In his autobiography,[16] the eleventh-century Benedictine monk Guibert of Nogent recorded what had happened to his mother. One afternoon, after she had fallen asleep, 'it seemed to her that her soul was going out of her body. After travelling along a gallery she came out onto a well.

Human ghosts appeared suddenly out of the pit. Their hair looked moth-eaten. They attempted to grasp her and drag her into the well', but a voice ordered them to let her go and they dived back into the pit. The woman asked God to replace her soul in her body. But before this could happen, she had to meet her deceased husband. She had long been anxious about his fate after death. Her husband explained how he was suffering for his sins, and told her what she could do to alleviate his pains. Then she awoke. The vision had answered her question, proved the existence of infernal creatures, and showed her God's mercy.

In a more sophisticated way, the Iranian philosopher Avicenna (980–1037), Guibert's contemporary, thought that our minds are freer at night than by day because we are no longer obliged to humour our limbs and organs. Only then, when our bodies are at rest, may we communicate with the supramundane world. Emerging into an universe more real than our ordinary environment, dreams are seen as revelations that, veiled during the day, are relieved of the predefined form of logical, orderly accounts, and thus invested with mystery and wonder. Dreams introduce us to another understanding of life, more symbolical, less cerebral and cognitive than the form of discernment we use when we awake. Macrobius mentioned an opinion widespread in the ancient world, according to which a veil, hanging over nature, separated humans from truth; it was in sleep that, sometimes, the veil was removed. Flavius Josephus, a Hellenized Jew and rational thinker of the first century AD, gave a smooth version of that liberation when he explained that, in sleep, 'the soul, untroubled by the body, but enjoying in perfect independence the most delightful rest, is able to converse with God, take a sight of the universe and foretell many things that will happen'.[17]

The liberation of the soul by night has long been a poetic common-place. Cicero, in his short *Scipio's Dream*, fancied that in a dream the Roman general Scipio Aemilianus flew over the earth and examined the planetary system. Countless medieval tales narrate how the Virgin or a

saint carried some devoted souls to another place where they accomplished urgent tasks or witnessed God's marvels. Hugo, in *The Sea Workers*, portrayed a character who believed that while earthlings were asleep, they were able to join the invisible inhabitants of space and play with them just as if the vague shadows we remember after waking up were real beings. Freed from their sleeping bodies, spirits visit mysterious places the writer dreamed of – and sketched – during his trip across the Pyrenees. William James, one of the founding fathers of scientific psychology, divided the universe into Nature and 'a spiritual world, actually an existing region of being' only attainable in dreams.[18] Pre-industrial societies often believed in the actual existence of spirits capable of materializing at night and showing themselves during dreams. At the end of the nineteenth century, the Ojibwa, a tribe of Algonquin-speaking American Indians, distinguished two kinds of beings, the human and the non-human, the latter able to manifest in dreams under the appearance of known living entities.[19] Even today, Siberians maintain that during a 'dream', which can sometimes last an entire week, the 'body' of a future shaman is dismembered: his organs are removed, and replaced by new ones.

Let us forget the imaginative side of these beliefs; what remains is the ontological question of how flesh and spirit interpenetrate in human beings. Summing up the core of the problem, Avicenna, neither a mystic nor a poet, described sleep as an eclipse of our cognitive faculties. While judgement was clouded, the imagination's visionary potency could blossom freely. This, of course, is pure speculation, like most dream theories. Our concern is not to decide for or against this view, but to remember what has been defended with equal confidence by various thinkers: some believe that in sleep our self is given over to the worse instincts; others, that it is liberated from the tyranny of the body.

A Deity, or our Imagination?

It has never been clear whether nocturnal life, separated as it is from material bonds, is of a purely physical nature, or whether it is a liberation of human inventive capacities. Is there a message involved in dreams? If so, how is it possible to know who sent it: our body? our mind? or some external source? Freud, anxious to advertise the novelty of his system, contended that, before him, dreams were seen as communications sent by some deity to predict the future, while psychoanalysis conceived them as mental productions likely to help disclose past traumas. Freud's influence is so pervasive that countless academics have unwittingly endorsed his opinion. It has been written, for instance, that 'from unnumbered dreams related in ancient literature it is apparent that everybody was convinced that dreams were messages from the gods'.[20] In fact, such a straightforward, uniform conception of dreams has never existed.

In the ancient world many doubted the divine origin of dreams. Aristotle, who was not alone in his opinion, admitted that dreams were of divine origin inasmuch as they were aspects of a nature created by the gods, but thought they had no purpose and did not emanate from a deity. He wondered what might bring the gods to send messages to humans and why they would communicate with ordinary people when it would be wiser to advise only those who were able to understand. He conceded that events represented in dreams came true afterwards. But, as he added, when we are planning an action we find ourselves so deeply concerned with it that 'the dream has had a way paved for it' from the project set up in the daytime. Cicero went even further. His short text *On Divination* was a lampoon against those who maintained that dreams could bring a divine revelation, since the gods, if they had some advice to communicate, would do it openly with signs less dim than the blurred images we see at night. Even during the Middle Ages it was sometimes claimed that dreams were 'internal' signs issued by the dreamers themselves, although there was no agreement about the sources of such manifestations. An interesting example of this ambivalent understanding of nocturnal productions can be found in the thirteenth century, when the introduction of Hippocrates' medical treatises of the mid-fourth century BC offered a completely physiological and somatic account of the process of dreaming. The *exclusively* natural origin of visions was condemned in Paris in 1277, but theologians continued to debate on the ambivalence of dreams, which could be both true and false, earthly and divine.

If we wish to make sense of the harsh controversies over dreams we must understand that in the past many people were unsure as to whether they should stick to one interpretation only. Herodotus, in his *Histories*,[21] reports four dreams foretelling a tragic event. He told of another dream so frightful to the Persian general who had taken and sacked the Greek island of Samos in the fifth century BC that the Persian hastened to make good the destruction.[22] It is therefore tempting to conclude that the Greek historian believed in the anticipatory power of dreams. However, all the previous anecdotes were reported very briefly, while a much longer text appears rather ambiguous.[23] In 480 BC, Artabanus, uncle of the Persian king Xerxes, advised his nephew not to attack the Greeks. But the king had two dreams urging him to take the offensive. Artabanus warned him: 'You say that you are haunted by a dream sent by some god who forbids you to give up the idea of the expedition ... Those visions roaming about us in dreams are for the most part the thoughts of the day; and in these latter days we have been very earnestly busied about this expedition.' Here Artabanus sided with Aristotle's views. Xerxes persuaded Artabanus to sleep in his bed with his clothes on; Artabanus had the same dream, and so consented to the expedition, which ended disastrously. Herodotus' story can be understood in many different ways: fear or weariness on Artabanus' part, the blindness of those who wear the royal insignia, a trick played by Greek gods. One thing is clear: according to the Greek historian, clever people do not trust dreams unless they know how to interpret them.

Their obscurity makes it possible to misread or distort dreams; countless examples show how individuals have long been trying to turn a dubious, or even an ominous, vision in their favour. A Babylonian hymn of the third millennium reads: 'Send me that I may see a favourable dream. The dream I see, may it be favourable. The dream I see, may it come true. The dream I see, turn it into favour.'[24] The Roman author Pliny the Younger, writing to his friend Suetonius, who was frightened because of a bad dream, warned that dreams might work by a contrary means, so that it was necessary to ponder whether in any specific case dreams predicted directly or in reverse. The archetype of this conscious play on the meaning of dreams is in Sophocles' *Oedipus Rex* (420s BC). A woman who has had an obsessive dream addresses a prayer to Phoebus Apollo: 'If it is a good omen for me, fulfil it; but if it is ill, may it fall on my enemies' (line 645).

Can we speak of duplicity or of bad faith? Synesius of Cyrene, a lucid thinker, explained why that was not the case. He noted that there could be no 'true' system of explanation since humans were different by nature: 'each person must hold themselves as material for the art. Let them inscribe on their memory the affairs in which they have been involved, and the nature of the visions that have preceded them.'[25] He added that divination must be taken seriously inasmuch as 'it comes from us, is within us, and is the special possession of the soul of each one of us'.[26] Imagination, transcending intelligence, helps people to contact higher realities, for instance to perceive the gods' advice.

Dreams never lie, Synesius maintained. But those who are not well trained or do not want to interpret their dreams are likely to misunderstand them. This is not too harmful: hope being the law of mankind, people need the anticipation of a better future in order to struggle on with life. During the night, many Greeks argued, sick or crippled people see a deity or a messenger of the gods, and are sometimes cured. Synesius did not take a stand on the intervention of a deity, and there is nothing surprising in such prudence. From time immemorial and in some countries today, people have believed in the curative powers of dreams. This is often labelled 'popular opinion'. Popular is correct if it means what is common to a great number of people, but not if it isolates uneducated people. All social strata were anxious to receive some divine help through dreams. *The Miracles of Artemios*, written in the seventh century AD,[27] lists 45 people who slept in the church of St John the Baptist in Byzantium and had a dream sent by St Artemios. Fourteen were priests, high dignitaries sometimes close to the emperor, ship owners, bankers or rich tradesmen.

The idea that there are dreams that are purely human and dreams sent to the dreamer 'from outside' by some ill-defined sender, a deity who prescribes something, or 'spirits' who provide a warning, was for a long time widely diffused and accepted. According to the Jesuit missionaries who lived among American Indian tribes in the seventeenth century and observed them closely, the Senecas, one of the Five Nations that populated what is now Ontario, paid much attention to their dreams. They saw individual dreams as expressions of concealed desires to be fulfilled, since their repression would cause mental or physical illness and could even result in death. Other dreams were created by supranatural beings and became a warning or advice for the whole community.

It is not difficult to understand why, in a society where faith was central, almost everyone thought that a message could arrive by night. For true believers who interpreted, and still interpret literally, the Bible or the Koran, no doubt is possible. In the latter (sura XII), Joseph's father explains that if dreams at times look incomprehensible, God will provide the interpretation when necessary. Muhammad's first victory over the city of Mecca was obtained after a dream in which God cheated on the prophet since, as the Koran relates (sura VIII), this was the Lord's best trick to persuade the Prophet to fight.

However, dream reading raises two more questions. The first is simple, at least for devotees (and it is worth remembering that two-thirds of us today live in places where religion is still a powerful force): how is it possible to decide whether a vision is of natural origin or has been sent by a deity? The other problem is far more complicated: setting aside the pressure exerted by the faithful, who did not want to give up their expectations, how can we explain why religious authorities endorsed the divine source of some dreams? Why is it, for instance, that Muslim dreambooks widely diffused in the seventeenth and eighteenth centuries insisted that only 'unbelievers' attributed dreams to internal humours, making thus the heavenly source of some dreams an article of faith?

It was never clear what distinguished a human dream from an inspired one, and the issue was complicated by the fact that bad spirits were likely to inject dirty images into sleepers' brain. St Thomas Aquinas defended the classical view that waking people were reasonable enough to resist Satan's temptation, but that by night, when reason was suspended, the arch-fiend was able to offer seducing pictures and thereby stimulate the imagination so that, being misled, people would consent to sin.[28] Discernment was therefore of vital importance: all religions tried to give criteria that boiled down to the idea that 'healthy' dreams could be divine. According to the Babylonian *Talmud* (early fifth century AD), dreams were blissful if they had a river, a bird or a jar – all stronger than destructive forces. Christian texts elaborated on what can be considered sanctified. The Muslim dreambooks mentioned above recognized three kinds of dream: some originate in the self and are motivated by materialist desires, such as food or sex; some are sent by the Devil; and some come from God, these being easy to identify since they are quiet and show only pleasant, honourable events.

Offering a clear-cut distinction proved impossible, yet few theologians would have conceded that it might have been better to forget dreams. We find here a privileged tool to differentiate monotheist religions from other cults: the former maintain that there exists another world, but how can we get in touch with it if not thanks to messages sent by night? St Thomas Aquinas stated that angels could carry instructions or blessings to sleepers.[29] Avicenna mentioned (without giving his personal opinion) a theory defended by important Muslim scholars. For them the images seen in dreams were not imaginary but real; they were perceived by 'another sense' and had an existence outside the subject. Avicenna's problem was the nature of life after death: spiritually advanced souls would then be illuminated, but what would happen to lesser believers or sinners? Pleasant or terrifying dreams made it possible to attest that there would be amusements for the former, physical pain for the latter.

Puzzling questions have played such an important part in the cogitations concerning dreams that I have found it necessary to explore them at some length. But what has been said could give the erroneous impression that these were obsolete preoccupations that vanished with the advent of a scientific study of dreams. This would be a mistake. Psychoanalysis is often likened to its main exponent, Freud. However, there was another leading figure, Carl Jung, whose influence is still strong in Swiss and East European medical circles. Initially Jung was a disciple of Freud, but he later broke away, contending that Freud overemphasized the importance of sexuality and did not perceive the everlasting value of symbols. Jung conceived of human beings as divided between a conscious side and an independent force. Though ignored by the conscious, the latter was an integral part of the self, able to feel and to act. Unlike Freud, Jung considered the force within to be a rich and diversified impulse, as important in our life and decision making as the conscious. In his view, our internal ego was manifested in slumber, and dreams reflected its activity. Some of these dreams were personal and caused by biological reactions or daily concerns. Others seemed incomprehensible, they were 'archetypal' dreams, universal patterns characteristic of the most common human problems, 'collective representations' forged by people for millennia. These were fragments of 'an immensely old non individual psyche' common to all humans, permanent in us and not modifiable. 'We cannot afford to be naïve in dealing with dreams. They originate in a spirit that is not quite human, but is rather a breath of nature.'[30] When people face a difficult problem, archetypes unknown to them but which are stored in their unconscious are reused to disclose the problem. Understanding what is an archetypal dream sometimes appears difficult. A good example might be Georges Perec's fantasy of a removable skull: *'Rubbing the nails of my thumbs on the edge of the bone I don't need to press for the bone to loose itself (like a watchcase or the plate which shields the battery of my radio set) and roll on the floor. I see my cortex. I pick up my bone and put it back.'*[31] This dream showed Perec something that no one can see. It was an unconscious, involuntary picture of his inward self made accessible because it is universal among people. In this Jungian scheme, a large portion of dreams is of collective, not individual, origin.

An Everlasting Enigma

In this chapter I have mentioned ancient texts more often than I have modern writings. Why refer to the Koran, the Bible, Plato and Aristotle, when since the mid-nineteenth century hundred of volumes have explored dreams? Because, despite countless experiments carried out in hospitals and universities, we are far from having a unified, consistent dream theory at our disposal. We encounter the problems our ancestors faced 4,000 years ago – and probably long before then.

Successively and simultaneously human beings have used myriads of dream interpretations, external or internal, optimistic or pessimistic, unified or dissociated. Dreambooks, which are still very popular in many parts of the world,[32] offer readings inconsistent with religious explanations that put forward the intervention of supranatural forces, as well as with contemporary systems that speak either of a power within us (the unconscious, more profound and sometimes stronger than our conscious mind), or of neurophysiological phenomena. Do dreams reveal the shameful part of ourselves, which is hidden behind the face we present to others? Do they reflect an individual's deepest self? Or is sleep a mere lessening of the sensory stimulus so that dream images, though enchanting, have nothing to tell us about ourselves?

We have been confronted with a wealth of answers at variance with one another. Starting from simple data, these schemes develop according to philosophical postulations and fail to result in a unified, undisputed procedure of analysis. This is not just because the workings of the human mind still elude us; it is more likely that it is because dreams involve a close relationship between the physical, the easy to observe, and the mental, the ineffable. Doctors and psychiatrists must rely on unverifiable statements for dream reports are the sole material at our disposal for the study of dreams. Are these accounts utterly spontaneous? Or do they follow socially established rules?

CHAPTER THREE

Dreamtelling: An Exercise in Rhetoric

To convey the main ideas of a dream does not seem difficult. Our normal dream experience is to 'see' or to 'hear' directly. Since our recollection is short-lived we are obliged, even if we merely want to report our dream to ourselves, to collect our thoughts immediately after waking and write down what we remember. Afterwards we shall be able to analyse our dreams and communicate them, thanks to the traces they will have left in our oral or written accounts.

Is this as easy as it sounds? Let us ignore the writer's skill, although it is likely to make a difference between a clear and a confused narration. Here is a very simple dream image: *'A means of transportation – a bus probably, everything is black, there does not seem to be anybody.'* The dominant impression is blackness, nothing frightening, only a sensation. What should be stressed? The strangeness of the 'setting' (*everything is black'*) or the expression of a sensation rather than a location? Or the conviction that the dream began in a public vehicle? In dreams there are things that are not ineffable and make themselves manifest, but which cannot be put into words. The *Miracles of Artemios*, the collection of incubation dreams mentioned earlier, vividly depicts the embarrassment of those who had slept in the church of St John the Baptist in Byzantium. There had been a presence, someone in their fantasies. Was it the saint? In the morning they felt confused, 'checked their dreams and thought that what they had seen was utterly imaginary'. Deciding what had 'happened' during the night is not straightforward. We are faced with several possibilities and do not know whether we must emphasize one specific point or leave the matter open. In fact, there is a wide fringe of indecision in many evocations. *'I am in London, in a distant district. I am with unknown people, maybe tourists, roaming in a drugstore. Encounter with another group. A vague feeling – I know them, they are, or might be, friends of mine. One of them is surely Jack, but he looks very different, I don't recognize the man, but I believe he is Jack.'*

Let us continue the dream of blackness and bus. *'A notice, I read – or I have the impression that I read: "Donnogan Castle"'*. Uncertainty about what was seen or heard and what was merely thought or faintly perceived is frequent. It occurs repeatedly in the accounts of two outstanding observers, Freud and the Victorian master of art commentary, John Ruskin. The former often noted: 'The woman said (there were not definite spoken words) . . .'. The latter, in his *Diaries*[1] (Ruskin recorded no less than 125 dreams), indicated that someone had said something. He remembered a sentence, but maybe there were only a few intelligible words. In one occurrence he 'heard' a music score: the melody was lovely and yet the vision painful. Quite often there was merely a feeling left in the morning. 'Dreamed the conceitedest and successfullest', but less relatable, dream. 'Dozed into the usual but not unpleasant dream which I forgot.' A strong effect was produced in the sleeper, but nothing expressible. The Austrian writer Robert Musil, another careful dream-watcher, conjured up in one of his novels, *Tonka*, dreams 'that were warm like low-roofed rooms painted in bright colours'. Parts of our dreaming is associated with unsettling impressions, flashes of light, colourful shapes, inaudible voices, whispering. Odilon Redon's drawing (over) of a sleeping man surrounded with

flowers evokes the fleeting, elusive images fluttering in a dream. Some observers seek the inexpressible and imagine procedures (likely to be transmitted by way of inarticulate sounds) that cannot be told in words. Commentators have always been baffled by a few verses of the *Koran* [2] that read 'Alif, Lâm, Mîm', etc. Muhammad perceived during sleep odd auditory enunciations that could only be expressed in onomatopoeia.

There is no explicit or even implied signification in such visions; they resist coherent phrasing. It is rather the rhythm, the kinetic effects, the affective involvement that are important, but dream reporters are at pains to formulate purely subjective sensations. 'You see, when I am tired, I don't know if it is for that reason, I often have strange dreams. For instance I often see a long shape, something like a cold, red or yellow flame which coils round me. And that, all night long, it's incredible. I don't feel frightened, no, rather upset.'

In such cases it is tempting to take a few concrete elements, a character, a location, in order to construct a narrative sequence that will sound odd but which evokes physical movements made while dreaming: *'A barking dog was in the centre of a gloomy room, it looked threatening. I was so frightened that I turned round, not on the floor but against the walls, up to the ceiling, as on a roller-coaster, at top speed.'* Or, in a less distressing way: 'In dreams I know that I am dancing, but I don't see either myself or the others. No image. It's, say, a whirl that carries us along and I am not here – but there is the swirl of all those who are dancing with me.' Some sensations, however strongly experienced, are, strictly speaking, *non*-sense, though we are aware of the fact that they sought to convey some sort of meaning.

Our initial dream of darkness and means of transportation goes on. *'Sit down, maybe it's the inspector who invites me to do it. I have got off.'* Images come one after the other at random, there are sudden changes of locations and characters. The narrator who seeks to recall as much as possible would like to organize the report and give it structure. Conjunctions help to join up impressions that, in fact, are not related. *'I find myself in Mark*

Lane (or is it Wardour Street? or Queen Anne Street?). I move from the back room to the living-room. Here is Jane (or is it Pat?). On the floor, chickens. Three of them or more. I take one of them and throw it outdoors – but there is no door, the whole house is crumbling, I can see the man who lives underneath, he is making a fire.' If there are different moments or different series of images in the dream just mentioned, the account tries to channel them into a consistent story. The 'jump' from the street to the inside is concealed by an imprecise 'I move'. From the street into the house or from one room to another? *'But there is no door'* links two visions (chickens; crumbling house) that may be totally unrelated.

Social communication is concerned with the transmission of messages. In order to make our ideas accessible to others we must arrange them. The intelligibility of what we say relies on the organization of our speech according to patterns that reduce the danger of misunderstanding but which channel and impoverish our thoughts. Any dream report is an exercise in language; a way of telling takes hold of the experience of the dreamer. If storytellers wish to deliver a message or to produce a strong effect on their listeners they choose a direct, highly stylized language. Think of George Fox, the seventeenth-century Quaker who was keen on astonishing his audience and used short, forceful sentences: 'I had a vision of a desperate creature like a wild hare or colt that was coming to destroy me; but I got victory over it.'[3] Such an account was based on what we might call 'the rule of the minimum'. It sought to tell only what Fox considered absolutely crucial, however absurd it sounded. To make the story coherent the narrator broke with the temptation of offering an elaborate, circumstantial narrative. On the other hand, some narrators (Freud, Jung) were so careful, or so full of their own importance, that they did not miss any detail.

Dream accounts raise the crucial question of what can be stated in a sentence and also of what cannot be expressed by a proposition. They do not form a 'genre', for they follow no formalist rules. They can be either lengthy or concise. The passage of time makes them change structure, details are forgotten, shifted or overrated, new parts are added. In short, they are unreliable, miss all that cannot be translated into orderly sentences, and merely provide a superficial idea of what was dreamed. Synesius of Cyrene remarked that 'in dreams, we conquer, we walk or fly simultaneously. Our imagination is able to cope with all that. But how will it be possible to find a verbal expression for it?' Why are so many so anxious not only to record their dreams but also to recount them?

'Don't Tell your Brothers'

After he had dreamed that the sun, the moon and eleven stars were bowing before him (Genesis, 37, 10), Joseph hastened to inform his brothers, who read the dream as a presage that he would dominate them, and they decided to get rid of him. In the Bible it is explained that Jacob, Joseph's father, was content with rebuking his son. The Koran (XII, 5) was more precise. More than a millennium elapsed between the first draft of Genesis and the composition of the Koran, but anthropologists maintain that a myth has no genuine version: later additions are merely amplifications of the initial scheme. According to the Koran, Jacob, after hearing his son, warned him: 'Don't tell your brothers the vision you had; they will set a trap for you.'

Telling other people one's dream may be dangerous, or at least tactless and unwelcome. If the dream is flattering to the dreamer, this fact is likely to offend the listeners and make them consider the narrator arrogant. If it is unfavourable the teller, put in an awkward position, will be despised. Even a seemingly impersonal dream can have serious consequences. The Roman historian Valerius Maximus reported that, in the fifth century BC, a Sicilian lady, having dreamed that she had been taken to heaven and advised of impending bad events, was all too happy to tell everybody her experience. Denys, a politician about to impose his dictatorship, 'was in a great hurry to eliminate her',[4] since she had said she could arouse his enemies' attention.

This anecdote by Valerius Maximus is revealing. We guess that the woman was proud of her dream. She had seen, in the house of the gods, something mysterious, something likely to interest her fellow citizens. There are those, Plutarch observed, who boast they have had important dreams, which make them think they are 'the favourites of heaven',[5] far above the common run. The 'impending bad events' of the Sicilian dream were not initially apparent: an exegesis was necessary. The desire for elucidation after most dreams is an urgent one. Many sleepers, like the narrator of Nerval's *Aurélia*, decide that they will attempt to 'set down the dream and get to know its secret'. The Jesuit missionaries who, in the seventeenth century, wrote copious, precise notes about the Indian tribes of Ontario, explained that whatever they had dreamed, the Iroquois thought it necessary to tell it as soon as possible, in order to obtain an interpretation. We do not know whether the Sicilian woman was personally frightened, but dream reports can tend to obtain a reassuring comment. In his version of Joseph's dream[6] (also an element of the myth), Flavius Josephus, the Jewish historian, alleges that the young boy, worried by his experience, recounted it to his brothers and asked them what they thought. Understanding perfectly well the meaning of the dream they did not tell Joseph and maintained that they were unable to offer an interpretation. Flavius, who was much interested in dreams and their meanings, reports other stories of people who, frightened by a dream in which they were killed or visited by a deceased person, in the morning hurried off to relate their hallucination and ask for a (comforting) exegesis.

Valerius Maximus gave precise details about the area of the heavens visited by his female dreamer. Was he a faithful reporter? Did he embellish his story? It hardly matters, for dream accounts are necessarily literary works. After carefully describing his dreams of competitions with his fellows, an amateur motorcycle racer confessed that 'It happens so quickly, I think I contrive as much as I see in dreams – but I like to tell it.' We have noted St Augustine's scruples: 'There still remains in my memory images of the things I used to do.' These were actions he would have liked to forget, but 'in sleep they are reactivated not only to my pleasure but also with my consent'.[7] The core of the problem, that which worried Augustine, was to know where the pleasure lay: was it in experiencing pleasure during sleep, or in remembering the pleasure after waking? Was is it not his lust that interfered and gave the dream report its vividness?

A gripping dream relation may be as pleasurable and diverting as a good novel. If it is told in public it is also likely to bring the narrator some fame. In simple, enclosed communities a dreamteller was often tolerated, even venerated or considered a merry *raconteur,* half chronicler, half liar. Investigations carried out among the Hopi tribes in the mid-twentieth century revealed cases of men who were used to gathering a small group around them and report their dreams, to the great delight of the audience. Three aspects of these accounts were of special significance. First there were frequent references to traditional beliefs or divinities such as the Water Serpent, a sometimes benevolent, sometimes threatening daemon whose hidden presence was familiar to the Hopi. Mentions of the Serpent rooted the story in a well-known, vaguely mysterious context, and, since the deity was much revered, guaranteed the accuracy of the message. Then, a few of the listeners were included in the story. More important, sexual hints were likely to provoke laughter. For instance an account began with men and girls swimming nude, an adventure totally unlikely to happen in the tribe. Or the dreamer would hide himself with a girl in a deserted house. Or a girl would jump into the dreamer's arms with her legs tight around his hips.[8] Though they doubted the accuracy of the report, the listeners were enthralled by a story that, under cover of a dream, offered salacious episodes.

The value attached to dreams in a society – the fact that they are considered as warnings, as symptoms of divine interventions, the knowledge of procedures of interpretation – all have serious implications for the community. Influential dreamtellers are spurred on to rework their dreams and emphasize the aspects that best suit their audiences, whether these include extreme guilt or self-confidence. Flavius Josephus reports[9] that when Alexander the Great entered Jerusalem, the high priest Jaddus was frightened, since the Jews had been loyal to the Persians, enemies of the Macedonian king. Jaddus made a sacrifice and went to sleep. The following day he 'announced to all the revelation that had been made to him' by God, who had instructed the Jews to adorn the city and make the king welcome so that, thanks to the Lord's protection, they would suffer no harm. The sailors crewing the ship that carried George Fox to the American colonies feared they would be stopped and inspected by the Royal Navy. Fox told them his dream of warships sailing far away in open seas, and they felt reassured.

A conjunction of local traditions, especially religious, and of favourable political circumstances can give a dreamteller an extraordinary influence. There have long been, and are still, visionaries in the Mediterranean islands. In 1822 the Greeks were about to liberate themselves from Ottoman rule. A nun, Pelagia, who lived on an Aegean island, had a dream. The Virgin Mary explained that she would like to have her house built in a nearby field. Excavations unearthed a well of holy water and an icon. The foundations were laid for a church that became one of the greatest pilgrimage centres in Greece. Not only did Pelagia succeed,[10] but she became a venerated nun whose premonitory visions were much sought after.

Dreamtelling will bring celebrity, contempt or hostility. However, fame is not necessarily the main spur. Coleridge did not report his dreams in order to impress his friends. His aim was to study the mechanism of imagination and explore the limits of his self. Private dream analysis may be a pleasing undertaking. Psychoanalysis has strengthened and legitimated the delight to be had in it, however insignificant the results may seem.

Psychoanalysts make the most of seeming trifles. For instance, a young lady tells one that in her dream she wanted to sit down in a lobby but was unable to because the armchair was occupied by her father. From this short account the analyst infers what her problems must be. If such a simple vision is considered significant, then all dreams can be meaningful.

George Devereux has published the proceedings of a psychotherapy in which the patient, a male Plains Indian, was asked to report his dreams.[11] Initially, the man had trouble in saying even a few words; his accounts were extremely short: 'I was butchering some beef.' The analyst showered him with questions in order to compel him to gather associations. Devereux is very brief on the strategy followed during the treatment, but one cannot help thinking that, by endlessly asking 'when, who, how', he supplied the man with the sketch of a correct report. The accounts soon grew in duration and scope: the man was able to talk at length, sometimes so quickly that Devereux could not follow him. The man realized that his words were of importance for the person he was speaking to, and he felt proud to have them recorded. When he had talked too fast, he even offered to repeat the whole story. Dream location, names, the status of the people in the dreams were stated clearly. Most accounts were in the imperfect, with short sentences in the present. For instance, after saying he had dreamed of people drinking heavily, he added 'I think to myself: *That's a hell of a way to do it.*' Where did such a comment come from? From the dream itself? Or was it superimposed in passing by a man who for a long time had suffered with a drink problem yet showed himself to be unforgiving in the case of other drunks? In his reports, diurnal anxieties were no doubt closely related to nocturnal thoughts.

Analysts are well aware of the process. They know that the presence of a silent witness will influence the patient. But they think that, when we call forth our hallucinations, we tend to expel their most unpleasant aspects. Only an external observer will press us to go into a topic that we would prefer to dismiss. What is important is not the letter of the dream but the associations it triggers, since every word may be telling. The case of Devereux's patient shows that, after a while, recounting becomes less difficult, and eventually pleasurable. Dream accounts have long been stylistic exercises likely to show to advantage the narrator's literary talent. According to Synesius of Cyrene, it would be extremely entertaining to publish people's dreams, with extensive information about their context. A collection of accurate observations would be beneficial and instructive. Yet, education was not Synesius' main concern; he assumed that a description of one's dreams would be 'a refined pastime' as well as a way of improving one's literary skill. Psychoanalysis has gone further and legitimated the power of imagination. Who can be sure that the embellishments lent to the report are not part of the dream, and vice-versa? Shortly after the publication of *The Interpretation of Dreams*, Freud wrote to his friend Wilhelm Fliess explaining that he was 'not an observer, not an experimenter'. He could have added he was, first and foremost, a great writer.

Vienna, 1900

Dream descriptions appear as a choice among several possibilities, not as an accurate and precise recognition of facts and traits. What matters is not the authentic dream that lies out of our reach, but the way it has been told. If any account were purely individual, comparable to no other story, dreamtelling would lack cultural importance, since we would be faced with myriads of idiosyncratic texts. It is likely, however, that some narratives conform to established patterns. Yet, the probabilities are neither infinite nor arbitrary. When we try to report a dream, be it silently, for ourselves only, we do it within a society of other minds linked to us by language and culture. Common sense suggests that idiom and education form our means of thinking and verbal expression, and accordingly, our dream reports. For instance, doctors who are used to precise diagnosis should produce dream accounts that are more brief and less literary than those undertaken by professional writers. Good sense produces hints, not proofs; its assumptions should be verified.

At the beginning of the twentieth century, Vienna was an extraordinary city, one rich in educated, cultured individuals busy exchanging ideas and projects. It was common then to keep a diary and to record dreams; reports were exchanged between friends. Thus we have a collection of dreams observed by three German-speaking doctors – Freud himself, the novelist and playright Arthur Schnitzler,[12] and the Swiss Carl Jung, who, though based in Zurich, from 1907 for several years frequently visited Vienna in order to work with Freud. Their notes provide us with the means to check whether dream reports conform to cultural patterns.

Freud and Schnitzler sought to bring out the dominant idea that could be detected in a dream. Sometimes this was merely a feeling, as when Freud told his fiancée, Martha Bernays, that, in a dream, he had 'the disagreeable feeling of being paralysed' when he was about to fight an aggressor (13 January 1896). More often a simple fact, a meeting, a fulfilled wish were selected. The accounts were succinct (two or three lines), words and conversations were not reported, nor were individuals or locations described. Before the publication of Freud's *The Interpretation of Dreams*, Schnitzler thought that dreams were disguised fulfilments of unconscious wishes, anticipating thus Freud's statements on the subject. And during the first decade of the twentieth century he did not modify his opinion. Schnitzler had read Freud's book as soon as it was published, but disagreed about the importance attached to sexuality. Did he have a mental blockage? At any rate he stuck for a while to his interpretations. On 23 March 1912 he noted in his diary that after rereading Freud he 'dreamed with an unusual neatness and limpidity'. It would take him a few more years, however, to venture a more personal analysis.

At the age of fourteen Freud had begun to keep a diary in which he noted his dreams, but he destroyed it in 1885. 'Irma's injection', the first dream he analyzed systematically, occurred on the night of 23–24 July 1895 at Bellevue, a house in the hills outside Vienna. It begins thus:

> 'A large hall – numerous guests, whom we were receiving. – Among them was Irma. I at once took her on one side, as though to answer her letter and to reproach her for not having accepted my 'solution' yet. I said to her: 'If you still get pains, it's really only your fault.' She replied: 'If you only knew what pains I've got now in my throat and stomach and abdomen – it's choking me.' – I was alarmed and looked at her. She looked pale and puffy. I thought to myself that after all I must be missing some organic trouble. I took her to the window and looked down her throat...'[13]

What strikes here us is the stylistic modification that occurred at that time. Instead of quick, synthetic notes, the 47 personal dreams described in *The Interpretation* are meticulously reported in considerable detail. Hence an important question. Did the new report technique reorient Freud's understanding of the 'dreamwork' (the dreamer's translation of latent content – the meaning that lies behind the dream – into manifest content – the dream as dreamed and reported)? Imagine 'Irma's injection' told in the previous, abrupt manner. The long, accurate description emphasizes details concerning not the general meaning of the vision but the way dreams work. Irma *'looked pale and puffy'*, whereas, as Freud pointed out in his analysis of the event in *The Interpretation*, 'my patient always had a rosy complexion. I began to suspect that [in the dream] someone else was being substituted for her.' Other particularities hinted at a sexual involvement. An exhaustive description purporting to be thorough analysis helped Freud to propose his hypothesis of displacement (one image symbolizes another image) and condensation (several images form a composite meaningful image). It is worth observing that once Freud had contrived these processes his successive work on dreams[14] resumed the initial, synthetic style. For instance: 'As part of a rather long dream a patient dreamt that several members of his family were sitting round a table of a particular shape.'

Are we to suppose that it was the study of scrupulous reports that resulted in Freud's coinage of new concepts? This would be far too simple. Freud stopped neither to control his dreams nor to consider very attentively the slightest variations in his patients' accounts. What did he do with all the material he collected over the years? Oddly enough he paid little attention to the structure of the dream narrative. 'Images' fascinated him more. In a footnote added to the 1909 edition of *The Interpretation*,[15] he apologized for having initially worked 'on my dreams which are usually based on discussions and conflicts of thought' and neglected the representations. What had changed after 1894 was the spread of visual impressions. Places first: *'The place was'*; *'I was in front of the station'*; *'a castle by the sea'*; *'a hill'*. Then the sleeper's position: *'I was standing'*; *'It was as though I was in the Aula'*; *'I was going to the hospital'*. People entered the scenes: *'I met one of my colleagues, P'*; *'Louise N. is working with me'*. The sharpness of the notes became impressive: *'My saddle was a kind of blister which completely filled the space between [the horse's] neck and crupper'*; *'The pelvis had been eviscerated and it was visible now in its superior, now in its inferior aspect, the two being mixed together. Thick flesh-coloured protuberescences could be seen.'* However, if there were a location, a few characters, an action, no attempt was made to correlate them. In other words, there was no 'staging' of the story.

Although Freud aimed to be both objective and accurate, and hardly hesitated to note trifles, his reports make easy, entertaining reading. They were well written, involved carefully chosen adjectives, staged in a few words a complex situation. It is difficult to believe that he was not enjoying the production of his descriptions. He did not omit the slightest element. He was scrupulous and pleased to find the right touch. In this respect he was at variance with his colleagues. Jung did not indulge in mentioning bizarre details. In his view, Freud collected them to provide the sexual clues he was obsessed with. Long or short, Jung's accounts look simple, direct, deprived of complications, as if his main concern had been to compose well-written papers, whereas his friend and master, Freud, became lost in trivialities. 'I dreamt that I was in my home, apparently on the first floor, in a cosy, pleasant room furnished in the manner of the eighteenth century', Jung recalls in one account.[16] We are far from Freud's short observations. Jung sets up a scene and reconstructs a chronology: *'I was astonished . . . I began to wonder . . . I found a door'*. He did his best to produce clear pictures, where Freud would have found composite images: there was *'a flight of stone steps that lead to a large vaulted room'*, *'the mortar 'was mixed with splinters of brick'*.

Are there two main models of dreamtalks, one progressing slowly, gathering on its way forward all that was seen during the night; and one heading steadfastly to its conclusion? Or, to put it diversely, one that gives greater scope to the infinite multiplicity of images and impressions, and one that pursues unity and simplification? Schnitzler's Diaries prevent us from indulging in hasty conclusions. He peppered his reports with parentheses, remarks or digressions and provided complementary information about people or places involved in his fantasies. Irony and distance helped him to avoid Jung's formal manner as well as Freud's meticulousness.

'In a train with Olga (and another woman? Mrs Bacharach?). Someone (who?) makes known that Mrs Zwerenz and Simons are in another carriage. During the journey Mrs Zwerenz leaves her compartment (sleeping room) in ball dress and enters, with her lover (who? he is not visible) in a kind of anteroom: she looks like (I only realize it on waking) Mrs Woivade. Meanwhile (?) Dr Kaufmann has given me his date-book on which are noted the evenings he has dinner with Bella (who, for the time being, is in Vienna).' (8 July 1913)[17]

While Freud or Jung attempted to give an exact description Schnitzler multiplied doubts and restrictions. But the main difference between the three doctors appeared where sensations – oral, kinesthetic or tactile – were concerned. Jung narrated without relating the physical or psychic impressions he might have felt. 'In one of my dreams a certain man was trying to get behind me and jump on my back. I knew nothing of this man except that he had somehow picked up a remark I had made and had twisted it into a grotesque travesty of my meaning.'[18] No mention of the fear or anger such aggression should have provoked. Freud 'saw' with acuity but was 'deaf'. Sounds are seldom noted in his reports. When noises are mentioned they are referred to external influences and never considered to be significant clues. Schnitzler affirmed that he 'heard' music in sleep in the absence of external sounds. He knew what the score was, and could even remember the passage. Music and smells played a significant part in his reactions; they provoked pleasure, distaste, anxiety. We find here a fundamental divergence in the understanding of the dream material that obviously affected our doctors' reports. Jung conceived of dreams as drafts or unfinished texts to be completed by the interpreter. Freud maintained that dreams disguised latent wishes. It was therefore urgent to track down all available signs in order to retrieve the dream's deep meaning. Schnitzler read his dreams as short theatrical performances, combining pictures, voices, tones, sounds and emotion.

'*I am playing the piano, A major as keynote, my partner is playing in A minor. People laughing (off the beat) – at the same time I see a rather wide framing which "in reality" is something else and modifies according to the piano music*' (1 July 1913).[19] What is impressive in these few lines is the synchronization, several events overlap each other. Are we not permitted to speak of a 'cinematic effect'? And to assume that Schnitzler, who was a film buff (he saw up to three films a week), modified his dream accounts in the 1910s under the influence of films? In a dream he met his wife in the doorway of their house. They talk. '*Then the framing disap-*

pears'. Here is another frame, a staircase, talk with beggars, a *'glimpse of the courtyard'* (6 July 1912). The successive frames are clearly delimited; all scenes are viewed from a different point of view, and at the end we have something like a shot taken from above. At times the cinematic reference is overt:

> *'Dream. I pay a visit to the Wydenbruck. Waiting in the lounge – there is a picture – the countess is seated in the lounge, I arrive from behind, steps, I arrive with a cigarette – it is really a pan-shot image . . . Too sad I have not brought my Zeiss [camera]. Then, again, from above, I see a mime show or a cinematic projection . . . Then a young man swimming – how many things cinematic actors have to perform.'*
> (6 August 1922)[20]

This reads like a film script. Successive 'shots', alternate close ups (picture, cigarette), long shots from above and camera motions. Compare Jung's report of his first dream: *'I saw before me in the dim light a rectangular chamber about thirty feet long.'* If there are landscapes, big rooms and people in Jung's dreams, his sentences are perfectly polished, whereas Schnitzler 'edits' a series of snapshots.

A thematic index of the fantasies reported by our doctors would catalogue the same topics: sex, family and friends, socialites met in evening receptions, trips in the country or in the mountains, domestic worries, health problems, banalities typical of bourgeois life around 1900. Yet, the glaring influence of the social and cultural context is of little importance. What makes these accounts fascinating is the authors' literary talent. I suggested earlier that dreamtelling helped to release nocturnal tensions and was a way of captivating an audience. I may now add the pleasure of finding an adequate expression not for our visions (any attempt to establish whether we really dreamed what we remember would be hopeless), but for our feelings. Dreamtelling is a pretext for self expression that is much appreciated in various societies, especially in Western countries.

The Temptation of Forgery

Some dream reports are enthralling, comic or fantastic enough to be interesting in themselves. The artistic quality of many accounts arouses the suspicion that uncoordinated images and vague sounds have been shaped into enticing stories held together by an artificial chronology and spurious mechanisms of cause and effect. Graham Greene had dreams filled with attempts at hiding or escaping, wanderings in dark side streets and inescapable policemen. When relating them, he emphasized a precise episode that gave his accounts full coherence. For instance, he stressed the fact that he was entrusted with killing Goebbels, the Nazi propaganda minister. However short and confused, his (failed) attack appeared to justify the long and chaotic divagations that followed. Greene was not a theoretician, and his tricks make his texts more pleasurable. Dreamtellers use various materials that have necessarily been reworked. What is the impact of the literary form given to these accounts? Will it give their content more accuracy or authenticity? Or will it influence and even determine the theories based on such observations?

Freud called one of his dreams 'the three Fates'.[21] In fact there are no Fates in it. He dreamed that he entered a kitchen, where he met three women. Later they made him think 'of the three Fates who spin the destiny of man' and he 'knew' that one of them 'was the mother who gives life'. This woman was *twisting something about in her hand, as though she was making Knödel [dumplings]*'. In his commentary Freud points out that this was 'a queer occupation for a Fate'. However, in the dream account, the woman is not a Fate. She is in a kitchen, apparently involved in some domestic duty. The account of the dream does not mention any question raised by Freud.

It jumps directly to the woman's reply. *'She answered that I must wait till she was ready . . . I felt impatient and went off with a sense of injury.'* Freud tried twice to put on an overcoat, and quarrelled with a stranger who claimed that the second overcoat was his. After a long and extremely clever analysis based on associations, Freud concluded that the dream in which 'vital needs announce their presence' was 'clearly a hunger dream' with transparent sexual hints, overcoats being generally used in nocturnal fancies to represent condoms.[22] The discrepancy between the report and its exegesis, dismissing, as the latter does, many details, has led Lesley Chamberlain to offer a different interpretation.[23] As a young man, Freud suffered a good deal of sexual frustration before improving circumstances finally allowed him, at the age of 30, to marry his sweetheart, Martha Bernays; the lady in the kitchen might be Martha herself, or her awkward mother, perhaps, making Freud wait for his sexual satisfaction.

Chamberlain's thought-provoking exegesis does not contradict Freud's analysis. Dreams are open to endless readings; Freud himself acknowledged that no investigation will exhaust the hermeneutic potential of dreams. The terms used in the account prejudge its exegesis, or rather preclude other possible elucidations. However arguable, I would like to suggest a slightly modified version of the dream without changing its manifest content. The words I have added (in many cases replacing Freud's) are those in roman.

Three Women

'I went *into* the *kitchen* to satisfy my appetite. *Three women were standing in it. One of them was* the hostess. *She was twisting something about in her hand, as though she was* twisting meatballs. *She answered that I must wait till she was ready. I felt impatient and went off with a sense of injury. I put on an overcoat. But the first I tried was too long for me. I took it off, rather surprised to find it was trimmed with fur.'*

I have just changed a few words without modifying the original meaning. Circumstances, characters and actions are perfectly equivalent. Freud is still wanting something. The woman is still the hostess. Yet the sexual nature of the story becomes so obvious that manifest and latent content now coincide perfectly. What I have made is pure forgery. But it is not an attempt to 'put right' the original. Freud's account and commentaries were part of his self-analysis. The vision was told in a manner that authenticated its interpretation. The text I propose is, in fact, another version, one that was not remembered and written down by Freud. It is therefore pointless to wonder whether the accounts that select and structure the material dictate the theory, or whether the accounts are a mere illustration of a pre-established theory. Interpretation and dream reports should be considered simultaneously.

The Awakened Dreamer

The difference between these two versions of 'the three Fates' is not limited to the interpolation of a few words. It lies also in the context. Dream accounts, like any verbal expression, must be replaced in their uttered circumstances. There is no means of checking how individuals felt when they woke up. Nor is there any possibility of knowing why awakened dreamers decided to remember and write down their experiences. But we can consider the most common condition in which dreams are told. Speaking and writing seem natural activities, but those who wish to communicate what has often been a very impressive experience must adapt themselves to the expectations of their audience. It is not unusual to read the following in anthropological works: 'Here is a dream recorded from a woman; in her dream the woman goes with a friend to the village spring for water etc.' Confronted with the questions of a foreign investigator, such a woman would have been obliged to set out very clearly what might have been imprecise in her mind. The researcher would then have translated the verbal account and written it down. What was initially present-at-hand would have become a less personal report channelled by predetermined rules.

Interviews are biased dialogues, one person feigning neutrality while the other is deeply implicated in what is happening. Signs of this imbalance are found in dream accounts delivered orally. A Greek papyrus dated to 161 BC[24] relates the dream of a Ptolemaios. The first sentence creates the impression that the man himself is speaking: 'I thought that [there was] a cow and that she was in birth travail.' But soon after we realize that another person has recorded Ptolemaios' words: 'He seizes the cow and puts her down. He inserts his hand into her vulva and draws out the bull.' Then the narrator returns: 'What I saw in the dream, may it be well for me.' The text we read is a transcription made by a clerk. Although very telling, it is about the nocturnal worries of Egyptian peasants, it is an elaborated duplicate of the original.

Let us compare two series of records collected in two entirely different periods. The first is the above-mentioned *Miracles of Artemios.* The second was collected in the 1970s by a French sociologist, Jean Duvignaud, who questioned more than 100 people.[25] The compiler of the *Miracles* used earlier documents, but also interviewed new patients. The former accounts describe briefly the illness, the dream and its outcome. The latter are much longer. The testimonies make it necessary to prove that they are reliable: 'A man said under oath . . .'; 'I saw in my sleep . . .'; 'Stephanos, a deacon, told what follows . . .'; 'The man is still alive and celebrates the saint.' Then come meticulous details, sometimes far removed from the dream, which tend to strengthen the validity of the report. Often we have the impression that particularities have been borrowed from the narrator's awakened experience: 'St Artemios came out of his shrine, got over the railings of the choir and came to me. He wore a baldric and had a stole around his neck.' It seems that the storytellers, anxious to please the chronicler or to meet his expectations, increased the interest of the miracle by accumulating details.

Duvignaud wanted to check whether there is a relationship between people's social-economic status and the content of their dreams. He was anxious to describe the situation of his informants, but did not care about the wording of their impressions. If he noted that a few groups, especially those threatened by economic development, were reluctant to talk, he failed to take into account the very peculiar exchange between interviewer and interviewee that may have led some people to remain silent. There were interviewees who did their best to retrieve a gripping dream: 'Four or five days ago I dreamt that my sister – she was under a lorry . . .'; 'If something frightens me during the day, if something has got to me, well, then, the night after, I have a dream.' As with the *Miracles*, but in a different context, there was a tendency to dramatize things: 'The nightmare, it lasted almost an entire day and I told it. Yes, that was all night long and even during the day. I couldn't get rid of the nightmare. . . . That was an obsession. Yes, I was upset throughout the morning and throughout the evening, I didn't know how to get rid of the nightmare.' When the dream had left a strong, but ill-defined, impression, it was completed by adjacent remarks:

> *'I am afraid of horses, I had seen horses, all day long, there were many horses, there were 25 or 30 of them, I was in a lane and all these horses, I let them go past me. Well, I was afraid of their legs and during the night I was caught there, I tried to fight to avoid these legs and I always saw horses legs, always legs and I suddenly woke up.'*

Duvignaud's analysis illustrates the pervasive influence of daily events in the reports of those not used to dreamtelling. But these people were interviewed by researchers who knew them previously; they may have been tempted to emphasize their ongoing concerns while missing other, less comprehensible, ones. This is not meant as a criticism of oral accounts, but merely to signal that they cannot be exploited without a good understanding of the circumstances in which they were delivered.

Since written reports are made by the dreamers themselves, the distortions are less obvious. Here again the context has to be pondered. We do not know to what degree private diaries are faithful reports, but we may suppose that they do not embellish stories, at least when they are not meant to be published (Schnitzler's *Tagebuch* was not to be published for 50 years following his death). Letters often show an unwitting desire to entice the addressee by means of an intriguing wording. Coleridge, who paid much attention to the content as well as to the meaning of his dreams, could not help giving a literary touch to his accounts of them. There was, for instance, an introductory note about his state of mind and the description of a debilitated old friend, so that after this dramatic glimpse 'I burst at once into loud and vehement weeping, which at length, but after a considerable continuance, awakened me.' Freud admitted: 'I might explain the part of the dream which I have not analysed; but I must desist at this point because the personal sacrifice demanded would be too great.' This is probably true of many accounts published in books.

For several months the author Georges Perec systematically recorded his dreams, but when he sought to have them published he had to cover up the proper nouns and cancel the evident allusions. Despite its flaws his collection is precious.[26] It reveals a neglected aspect of dream accounts, which is their purely emotional side. Some of Perec's notes are dry and purely factual, as if the narrator felt uninterested and wrote as a matter of routine. There was a train, a talk with the customs officer, a visit to the empty dining-car although all the seats were taken, children playing on the bar stools. The shorter accounts reveal indifference. Conversely, other reports display excitement or confusion, agitation, worry or pleasure. The sentences are alternately abrupt, limited to a few words or carefully elaborated. Present and past tenses mingle. *'All of a sudden I realized there were wet blots on the fitted carpet of my living-room. Maybe the cat. I feel, I smell: no smell. But there are many. I entered the kitchen.'* Colours, sounds, smells interfere, objects change shape and nature. The mental tumult is so powerful that instead of controlling what he was recording, the author wrote down the impressions as they came into his head.

Perec obliges us to reconsider the mental condition of those who collected their dreams. Then, seemingly insignificant clues reveal that many dreams were registered in a state of great tumult. It is, for instance, of little interest to read that the medieval chronicler Guibert of Nogent often woke up panicking and screaming. But the detail becomes meaningful as soon as we remember that, in this particular condition, he recorded dreams he had of the Devil or of dead people. The problem is not to decide whether Guibert was liable to nightmares. This is something we shall never know. What matters is the impact his daily anxiety had on his writings.

Ruskin used to describe his mood on waking. At times he felt so restless or so low that he cared little about recording his dreams. To a large extent the precision of his accounts is a barometer of his morning temper. On the other hand, Katherine Mansfield, when quiet, was content with dashing off a few words regarding the dominant theme of her vagaries. 'I *dreamed* a short story last night. It was very light. I dreamed it all – about children. I got up at 6.30 and wrote a note or two because I knew it would fade. I'll send it some time this week. It's so nice'.[27] But on troubled mornings she intermingled her nocturnal impressions and her awakened feelings. 'I went to sleep. And suddenly I felt my whole body *breaking up* . . . A long terrible shiver, you understand . . . When I woke up I thought there had been a violent earthquake. It slowly dawned upon me – the conviction that in that dream I died.' In contrast to such melancholic accounts, a pleasant morning mood is often

linked to the presence of beloved relatives or friends in dreams. Schnitzler's accounts bubble with joy when, in a dream, he happened to catch sight of his son or of a woman he cherished. Ruskin, often so morose at dawn, devised poetic dream descriptions that included elegiac landscapes and gentle animals if his cousin Joan had appeared in last night's dream. Writing what is remembered helps to distance oneself from the strong impression, good or bad, dreams can leave. Dreams, either frightening or enthralling, take us into a world that is not our usual one. Drawing or writing about them allows us to reshape our visions according to the rules of articulated narration. Gustave Doré's wood engravings for Edmond About's novel *The King of the Mountains* (1857) exemplify the pleasure found in calling up night fancies. Kidnapped by Greek brigands, together with an English lady and her pretty daughter, the protagonist kills time by sketching his fantasies of escaping with the young lady (see above) – but without the mother!

Description Patterns

Any dream narrative is delivered within verbally or visually organized forms of description. When talking about dreams we generally neglect the fact that in any given society the dominant language and the accepted forms of expression weigh heavily on the accounts. Specific words and structures determine not only the format in which the dream will be reported, for they have an influence on the dream categories considered or overlooked. In French and in Greek two different words mean 'dream'. The French distinguishes the light, superficial dream from the deeper one. In ancient Greece the coexistence of two terms affected the conception of nocturnal visions. In Book XIX of the *Odyssey* we find an opposition between confused, illusory mirages and serious visions that will be realized. Later Artemidorius, the famous soothsayer, formulated the same division on a linguistic basis. In his *Interpretation of Dreams* (I, 2) he contrasted meaningful dreams likely to bring a message and trite ones that told little, if anything. Adopted by the Romans, accepted during the Middle Ages, the Greek tradition lasted at least two millennia.

According to their respective languages, Germans, Spaniards and English-speaking people 'have' dreams; Italians and the French, however, 'make' dreams. In Russian *son* means simultaneously dream and sleep. To have a dream is thus to see something in sleep. The expression 'to see' a dream was common in the ancient Near East and indicated a passive attitude, in contrast to the active one expressed in the Bible or in Greek texts, where divine visitors and their humble host move and talk. Typical Egyptian dreams read: 'Slumber overcame him at the moment when the sun was at the zenith and he found the majesty of the august god speaking with his own mouth as a father speaks to his son.'[28] In the 'Dream of the Pharaoh Djoser', 'While I was sleeping in life and happiness I found the god standing before me. I conciliated him with praise and offered prayers in his presence. He revealed himself concerning me with a friendly face.' The Old Testament accounts take up a different attitude, apparent in the first vision it reports (Genesis, 20, 3–6): King Abimelech abducted Sarah, Abraham's wife; in consequence of this, God 'came to Abimelech in a dream by night' and threatened him with death. Abimelech spoke in his own defence, but God remained unmoved, and Abimelech was forced to restore Sarah to her husband.

The structure of any language and its available vocabulary have long channelled the imagination of dreamers and diviners, thus creating dream-types. Reports conforming to these pre-established patterns have never proved to be the only possible ones, but have necessarily been more welcome and better understood than discordant ones. Many dream accounts are characterized by their conformity to accepted forms or ideas, not least because in their construction they appeal to the community and are therefore taken seriously. A few case studies will exemplify the functioning of the accepted models and illustrate their strength.

Given the dual conception of dreams dominant in antiquity and prolonged during the Middle Ages, how was it possible to distinguish a significant vision from an uninteresting one? The common answer, related by Artemidorius (IV, 76), was that there should be unequivocal attributes and characteristic features to identify the messenger. We must recall a linguistic trait mentioned in the introduction. In Greek liteature, dreams often 'visit' a person or, sometimes, they appear at the sleeper's head. When Penelope has her first vision in the *Odyssey* (IV, 795), a phantom enters her bedroom, engages her in conversation and then leaves. In its formulaic version the Greek dream was a little scene. The appearance of the guests was described in such detail that the sleeper could not help but recognize them. Cicero, sceptical about divine communications, parodied the standard model in *Scipio's Dream*, where the vision unfolded like an acted story. Scipio came first to talk to his grandson. Then a series of friends interfered, some speaking so loudly that they were about to awaken the young Scipio. The grandfather asked them to remain quiet and showed his grandson the world as seen from the sky.

We shall never know what people saw, but many accounts attempt to prove that the visitor – God, angel or saint – could be identified, and that he had performed his duty. Our main source is the report of miraculous, soothing visions in Aesculapian sanctuaries or later in churches. When the visitor was not clearly a deity he was described as an important personage. He appeared, for instance, 'as a man of rank' or he 'looked like a senator'. He could also adopt the features of a doctor or a nurse who touched the sick parts of the body or told the patient what he ought to do. Was this pure adherence to pre-established patterns? Is it not possible to think that sufferers were longing for an apparition, that they had a dream, and that, in their report afterwards, they turned their dream into an antecedent model?

The existence and spread of archetypal dreams is unquestionable. Flavius Josephus mentioned the vision of one of his contemporaries, Archealus, ethnarch of Judaea, who 'saw nine tall and full-grown ears of corn on which oxen were browsing'.[29] The reference to Pharaoh's dream of 'seven ears of corn . . . rank and good' devoured by 'seven thin ears . . . blasted by the east wind' (Genesis, 41, 1–8) is manifest. Was Archealus so familiar with the Bible that he was unconsciously influenced by dreams reported in it? Or did he choose to shape his account according to the biblical model? Deciding whether such description corresponded to an actual dream is beyond us. Here again is the uncertain difference between a nocturnal vision and its daylight report.

What emerges from Flavius Josephus' book, however, is that this particular recording followed the requirements of current dream accounts and remained within the limits of the acceptable. Regardless of his personal intentions, Archealus accomplished a necessary action by making his report. There were dreams whose enunciation went with a social or political event. I have already mentioned the vision of the Greek nun Pelagia. Examples abound in medieval and modern literature and conform to a pattern that is unlike the divine apparitions just touched on. Let us consider the case of the 'invention' of the Cross. Helena, Emperor Constantine's mother, was establishing churches and monasteries in Palestine when a dream told her where the Cross had been buried. The dream, as later reported, consisted of a disclosure (the Cross has not been lost), information (it can be discovered there) and an injunction (unearth it and build a church). The vision was both a sign and proof. In the countless circumstances where relics were located through information transmitted in a dream it is impossible to disentangle the initial communication from the later authentification. St Augustine, in one of his sermons concerning the finding of St Stephen's corpse, considered the revealing dream as both sign and confirmation. Hence the obligation, even in nineteenth-century Greece, to conform to the archetype. What would have happened if Pelagia had not reported her dream? No one knows. But insofar as she did, there was only one possible means.

Ancient and medieval literature abound in dream accounts that follow the two patterns described above. Should we suppose that many dreamed, or at least recalled, their visions according to these models? How much did social conventions weigh on individuals? Another unanswerable question. All we can say is that there were other ways of recording dreams similar to contemporary methods. Synesius of Cyrene opted for short sentences. Talking about a vision – important, because it confirmed his ideas that dreams help to remove a doubt – he was content to say that a vision inspired him to remain where he was, an injunction that turned out to be the best possible one on that occasion. On the other hand, thousands of confused statements attempted neither to develop a precise idea nor to stick to a model. Here are a few lines borrowed from a Greek papyrus of about 150 BC found in Egypt: 'I thought that I was in Alexandria on a great tower. I had a beautiful face and I did not want to show my face to anyone because it was beautiful. And an old woman sat beside me, and there was a crowd from the north of me and from the east. They cry out that a man has been made into charcoal and he says to me: "Wait a bit and I'll bring you to the divine spirit Knephis in order that you may worship him."[30]

Though different, the last texts, taken together, illustrate the limits of dream studies. It would be extremely rewarding to form a general theory explaining the construction of plots, the interference of motives and the articulation of images and sounds in dream accounts. Unfortunately many reports fail to conform to the theory. Dreams are only accessible through descriptions. What would be a good description? An account shaping a continuous story and making sense of scattered impressions, as found in Jung or Greene? Short sentences directed at the most important points, as found in George Fox or Synesius? The channelled reports favoured by Greek, Roman and medieval authors? The diffused sensations expressed in the Greek document cited above? Freud favoured this last type. What I attempt to show is that a careful, exhaustive account is no more objective than any other form of report. In fact, as we have seen, many different reasons lead people to relate their dreams: narrators are strongly influenced by their culture; particular circumstances weigh heavily on the shaping of oral or written descriptions.

What is felt, and perhaps seen, at night is far from clear. It is not new to state that the ways in which our dream accounts relate to the dreams themselves is uncertain. In a philological study of Joseph's dreams (one more version of the story) Philo Judeus observed that the words used by the young man were 'the utterance of one at a loss, hesitating, dimly supposing, not seeing steadily and distinctly',[31] either because Joseph could not remember exactly what he had seen, or because he could not find the appropriate terms. Spoken or written language, being a tool of public, relational activity, is not adapted to the expression of internal feelings or impressions. Marlow, the narrator in Joseph Conrad's bleak novella *Heart of Darkness* (1902), made this perfectly plain: 'It seems to me

I am trying to tell you a dream – making a vain attempt, because no relation of a dream can convey the dream-sensation, that commingling of absurdity, surprise and bewilderment in a tremor of struggling revolt, that notion of being captured by the incredible which is of the very essence of dreams.'

Yet these inadequate accounts are our only access to our sleeping life. Without them dreams would at best be mysterious, baffling impressions. Reports tend to link our fleeting sensations to our daily experience. Throughout descriptions we create a dream-world. This verbal universe, possibly very far from the actual experience of dreams, has been created by hundreds of successive generations and is perpetuated by our contemporaries. Let us now attempt to explore it.

CHAPTER FOUR

Exploring the World of Dream Reports

Every morning countless people report their dreams to their family circle. Sensations deprived of clear meaning, forms, sounds, colours are translated into short stories. Words tame fanciful impressions and make them comprehensible. Modified, and to some extent impoverished, what was neither concrete nor well-defined enters the realm of told dreams. Once related, our dreams seem less uncanny. If few are able to imagine new tales, all have strange dreams, and may arouse a passing curiosity in others by recounting them.

'Dreams are the children of an idle brain begot of nothing but vain fantasy', Shakespeare says in *Romeo and Juliet*. Some scientists also consider dreams meaningless. In daytime, they claim, countless unimportant details are forced into our minds by circumstances. For instance, while driving, we concentrate on the traffic but also register, unwittingly, sounds, flashes of light, the shapes and colours of cars and trucks. At night our brains must clear away such useless detritus; thus is the function of dreams. One physiologist has compared dreams to the cleaning of a recorded tape.

After we have sat and chatted with friends, we quickly forget what seems to us to have been irrelevant in their conversation and retain only what interests us. Similarly, dreams 'delete' unnecessary memories. Dreams have no purpose, they merely reactivate fleeting memories. However, the strongest impressions resist erasing. In the morning, a few images linger in our minds. Around them we weave short stories because – one scientific argument continues – catching people's attention with vivid, emotionally intense reports is far easier than captivating them by reporting confused impressions. The precision of our accounts develops markedly as soon as someone takes an interest in them. Purely idiosyncratic dream reports, the sceptics argue, say more about a person's imagination than about dreams.

The Puzzle of Dream Content

There is no way of testing, confirming or falsifying this thesis. The relativist point of view precludes any investigation about dreams and therefore appeals to those wary of all-encompassing systems. But as we saw in previous chapters, dreams and dream interpretation play an important part in many philosophical, religious and scientific theories. It would be difficult to maintain some systems if dreams were proved to be without significance. The *Roman de la Rose*, a thirteenth-century French romance, reveals the dilemma by confronting two incompatible statements. One of the characters, 'Nature', using the same terms as modern sceptics, reduces dreams to traces of the sleepers' waking preoccupations. But 'Reason', another figure, emphasizing dream's theological signification, refutes that idea vigorously: at night our souls, disengaged from bodily functions, are receptive to divine influence. It is then that God can impart to us knowledge of superior realities.

Debase dreams, and the divine messages mentioned in the Bible become meaningless. Likewise, psychoanalysis, at least in its Freudian and

Jungian versions, is deprived of its favourite material. How is it possible to restore to dreams a scientific status? Arguing with the sceptics, Freud maintained that dreams have a psychical value, but admitted that he could not give any demonstration, since his own assumptions were 'quite arbitrary'.[1] The only response to doubt is that dreams, while made of idiosyncratic images particular to every individual, deal also with issues common to us all. Those who take dreams seriously have long emphasized the existence of universal themes. However far we look in the past of dream studies, we find attempts to define general categories. Our oldest documents, dating from the Babylonian empire, have dreams in well-defined categories, such as death, work, sex, family, etc. These are still used in modern interpretation treatises. Strikingly, for over 4,000 years, humans have not only taken dreams seriously but have also attempted to prove that they are both personal and collective, some being shared by all people in any given period, and perhaps at all times. Freud himself found it necessary to stress the recurrence of a limited cluster of dream patterns. The themes frequently mentioned by most of his patients included the impression of being naked in public, the death of a loved one, strange sensations, such as flying or falling, and distressing situations, for example, losing a tooth or endlessly taking an examination. A very frequent dream theme was that of the railway station, the sleeper arriving at night on the empty platform out of breath from running and seeing the express's tail-lamp fade on the horizon. According to Freud, these were 'typical' visions. Almost anyone could fancy them alike, and their meaning was identical for everyone.

We do not know how dreambooks were understood in antiquity. Even today, when these manuals still sell well around the world, we cannot tell how they are really 'read' by our contemporaries. Yet, we may suppose that after consulting them, many feel relieved, since they make all delusions seem very commonplace. Countless dreams, however bizarre, have been catalogued and can be deciphered. Dreambooks aim at offering interpretations. Set thematically, they also provide the framework of a contents analysis.

Endlessly reissued and modified since ancient times, these books have strongly influenced dream studies. Both Freud and Jung read them carefully. Their style is extremely particular. It is generally what we might call a 'telegraphic' writing – brisk, matter-of-fact, and concerned mainly with one precise object or event: bodily functions, manufacturing, or handling of objects and tools. Other sentences are about entering or leaving a city, visiting a church or public building, doing errands, buying sheep or goats (in antiquity) or cars or television sets (today). Several kinds of food, characteristic of any period's diet are noted. The enumeration becomes at times purely mechanical, shifting for instance from the eating of animals to cannibalism, then to the eating of corpses and finally to the devouring of parts of the dreamer's body.

When reading these influential collections of brief accounts it is difficult not to think that dreams often deal with very ordinary situations. If the combinations of images or sounds involved in dreams are, in theory, unlimited, the range of imaginary circumstances does not appear very great. Many specific cases described in ancient dreambooks seem curiously unchanging, and have been literally transcribed in the interpretations circulated down to the present day.

If people all have the same dreams, is it not possible to order their visions according to a good, simple typology? Many attempts have been made to find a convenient, elegant classification system. Philo Judeus, a biblical exegete, proposed three categories. At one end were the messages sent from outside (God, in Philo's view); at the other were the dreams provoked by the individual, who, in sleep, resolved urgent problems. In between were unimportant, casual and at times confusing visions. Macrobius, a cool-headed individual, distinguished dreams actually or potentially conforming to reality, and enigmatic dreams that 'concealing with strange shapes and veiling with ambiguity' their true meaning required interpretation. Contrasting pairs have been favoured by most theoreticians. There were, for instance, active visions (the sleeper plays a part in the dream) versus passive ones (the sleeper is content with receiving a message), external dreams (the message comes from outside) versus internal ones (nocturnal vagaries created in the mind), symbolic dreams (Penelope, in the *Odyssey*, dreams that an eagle kills geese: the eagle symbolizes Ulysses, the geese her suitors) versus realistic dreams (I fretfully dream that I shall miss the train).

Hundreds of ingenious but irrelevant systems could be added. Let us consider Artemidorius' sophisticated categories. In chapter Three I alluded to his classification under two main types: dreams caused by mental worries or physical torment on the one hand; dreams that can help to determine the future on the other. There was no difficulty with dreams provoked by inward causes, whether from the soul's waking thoughts or the body's disposition, Philo, Macrobius and most specialists agreed with such a category. Many who are hungry or thirsty will, while asleep, imagine they are searching for food or drink, and even have found them. A person who is expecting an important event – whether beneficial or disadvantageous – will easily fancy in sleep that it has or has not happened. But defining 'prospective dreams', visions with outward causes, was highly problematical. Artemidorius found it necessary to divided them into five sub-categories. Since these were not sufficient, the soothsayer had to contrive newer sub-categories to crosscheck all occurrences. As dreams consist of visual imagery, narrative sequences, passing impressions and kinesthetic-affective embodiments, it is almost impossible to reduce them to straightforward, unambiguous situations. Let us consider a short, simple account:

'I go through a door from one courtyard to another. Everything is black, but it isn't night. In the second courtyard I see my friend Pamela who died two years ago. She is wearing a white dress. I hesitate between thinking it is a ghost or she is back with us (I am not sure: do I doubt she can be here, or do I waver from one idea to the other?). By asking banal questions about her health I try to have her tell me whether or not she is real. From

the first courtyard, my friend John calls: "You know she is dead." I can't find any trace of the previous day in this dream, I haven't seen John for ages. He did not know Pam and I have never told him about her. Does Pam's presence, the door between two different spaces, the presence of John who is a true believer, hint at death? But what about the white dress? Is it not the colour of life? And why a warning last night about death more than at any other time?'

I do not wish to analyse this account. I am not an dream interpreter; a serious exegesis would require relevant information about the sleeper. I am interested only in the relation content. At first sight the latter belongs to the 'meeting with a dead friend' series inserted in all dreambooks. But the encounter with Pamela is a small part of the story. There is also John's call (category: warning coming from a friend), the door and the two courtyards (category: going from one place to another), the black background that is not night (category: contradiction). And the final comment ventured by the dreamer is also an element of the text. In this banal, perfectly linear report there is neither a clear message nor a dominant figure. Only literary visions found in plays, novels or films conform to the well-defined categories described by dreambooks.

We noted earlier in Graham Greene's accounts a relative lack in apparently 'non-logical' elements and a permanent search for rational order. Yet the novelist could not totally obliterate sudden changes in his dreams. One night Greene fancied he was associated with a group tracking guerillas led by the poet W. H. Auden. The latter, who had been hidden, suddenly appeared, bleeding from wounds made by the novelist Evelyn Waugh. Greene struck Auden with a knife. Apparently unhurt, Auden began a literary discussion. Invited to a party, the authors compared the respective advantages of life in Britain and the United States. Auden preferred the latter. Greene hoped that Auden would make an important discovery. Both agreed on drinking whisky. Most dream accounts, like Greene's, borrow vividness from the invading presence of changing characters, objects and places. A train of images dealing with a particular theme leads to a different series of thoughts or is even interrupted and substituted by other associations. Who could decide whether Greene's relation hints at death, subversion, literary rivalries, intellectual friendship or merely drink?

The Remains of the Day

Those among the sleep experts who think that dreams form at random and convey no information take advantage of this diversity. According to them, dreams reveal a clear continuity with waking life. Unsystematically translating into short images sequences of personal events, they merely protract wishes, tendencies and apprehension of our conscious existence. As members of a society and part of a cultural context, our dream material, deriving from daily activities and concerns, is fragmented and reworked according to the literary, narrative and visual processes typical of our own epoch. At best they provide hints about how to cope with conflicts and our attitudes towards them.

Specialists agree on one point only: our dreams incorporate many reminiscences from our waking lives. To do otherwise would be absurd, since we have all experienced the incorporation into our dreams of headaches, domestic noises, alarm clocks or insistent worries. We are dreaming of a car drive. Horns start blowing in the street. We imagine a traffic-jam. We must stop. Caught between other vehicles our car cannot move. External noises have found their way into an ongoing vision. Around our perceptions we weave new episodes springing from the images previously formed in our mind. Had we dreamed of a train, the sounding horns would have been an engine whistle. As we do not want to awake we force nuisance, physical uneasiness, causes of anxiety into our dreams. Gérard Grandville, who considered dreams mere linkings of images, explained how they combined elements formerly perceived. His *Walk in the Sky* follows the visions of a woman who perceives the moon during sleep (see opposite). She associates it with familiar crescent-shaped forms, mushrooms, an umbrella, an owl, bellows, hearts, a bobbin and needle, a cart.

Observers have long mentioned the relationship between dreams and diurnal concerns. Three thousand years ago a cuneiform Assyrian document pointed out the influence affliction or apprehension has on sleep, concluding that they would necessarily result in bad dreams. Ancient literature was full of dreams caused by emotion, wish-fulfilment or sorrow. Asleep, Penelope fancied what she would like to happen: Ulysses was in her bed, 'in the flesh' and not deceptively (*Odyssey*, XX, 89–90). Conversely Dido, upset by Aeneas' imminent departure (*Aeneid*, IV, 465–74), saw at night what she dreaded: finding herself alone. Cicero's *Scipio's Dream* is a good essay on the relationship between diurnal activities and dreams. Cicero imagined that, on his arrival in Africa, young Scipio had a long meeting with king Massinissa, who was acquainted with his family. Very tired, he fell into a deep sleep and dreamed that his grandfather, Scipio, was standing before him. This, Cicero explained, was caused by his trip and recent talk with the king, 'for it happens quite often that our concerns or our discussions react upon us in dreams'.

The ancient gods themselves were aware of the distinctive feature of dreams. Wanting to warn Nausicca (*Odyssey*, VI, 13), Athena, in a nocturnal apparition, assumed the likeness of a young woman and talked about housework. The goddess was well advised. Except when they slept in a sanctuary, praying to be cured, the ancients seldom dreamed of a deity. Today, as in the past, many seen at night are not the Prince of Wales or the U.S. President, but those with whom the sleeper is involved in ordinary life. Most visions related on waking display a variety of minute details borrowed from ordinary occupation or pastimes. Here is what a seven-year-old girl reported:

'In my dream I wanted to swing. The seat of the swing was made of wood. It hung on ropes from an arm of a pear tree. I tried to get on the seat, but it wouldn't let me. It kept tipping me off and hitting me on the bottom. I needed to go. I sat on a log to play with flowers. The log was wet from last night's rain. I knew you musn't sit on damp things or you'll get rheumatism. I couldn't make it to the toilet in time. I hitched up my dress. Then I thought I had finished, but I hadn't.'

The notes on the swing and its rope, the remarks about rheumatism may have been added to please the parents. But the child remembered essentially her ordinary amusement, and right from the beginning, with the swing, the seat she could not immobilize, humidity and other details, incorporated an increasing bladder pressure into her fantasies.

Shall we say that children's fancies are unsophisticated? Adults also relate dreams inspired by recent incidents, secret hopes or fears. A keen walker, Ruskin brought back, while he was asleep, his long strolls: *'dreamed I was going up a lovely mountain ravine'*; *'dreamed of walk in which I took all the short-cuts over the fields'*. James Woodforde, an eighteenth-century English parson, fulfilled his desires in dreams: *'I dreamed last night that I was at an entertainment given by Mr. Coke at his house, among other dishes there was a faun roasted but cold, and plenty of hares roasted. Mr Coke very civil to me.'*[2] Georges Perec was more prosaic. He saw his cheap rented flat crumbling, radiators falling down, and apologized to the owner for the damage by transferring the responsibility to others. Or he had visits from office colleagues, but did not feel pleased and was afraid of being disturbed by others. This is merely a sample from a wealth of ordinary matter-of-fact accounts.

The grubby preoccupations of mundane life confront dream theorists with a serious problem. Whatever its premises, a general scheme must elucidate all aspects of the subject. If the worse part of our self manifests itself at night, or if some deity attempts to send us a message, if our liberated soul leaves its fleshy prison or if ancestral archetypes are disclosed in our sleep, why should we fancy walks in the country or radiators falling down? Only elementary systems such as Heaven / Hell can provide a clear-cut answer. Devout Christians, for instance, will affirm that the Devil made James Woodforde lust after roasted hares and a squire's friendship, but such explanations are of little help. The problem cannot be easily dismissed. Freud was honest enough to tackle it, but the little he said shows how ill at ease he was.[3] He labelled the diurnal traces 'day's residues,' making them look like mere leftovers. In his view these were 'some cheap material always ready to hand' and totally different from the 'precious material' forming the latent content of dreams. The latter material prescribed the general organization of the dream, aimed, as we have seen, to fulfil a secret desire. The dream-work employed 'day's residues' whenever this was needed. However, Freud did not explain why at times the recourse to trivia was necessary. Implicitly, he endorsed a view common to most dream specialists: echoing our ongoing preoccupations or our physical uneasiness, a great many dreams are of little significance.

Sceptics who consider dreams unimportant stress the general agreement on trivial, 'cheap' daytime remains that infect our dreams and sometimes colonize them entirely. This, they argue, demonstrates how during sleep we rid ourselves of unproductive images or impressions stored by day. There is more. Our visions are mere reflections of contemporary cultural trends and common interests. Current vocabulary and images include colloquialisms supplied by the relator. When, while dreaming, Georges Perec saw his skull, it looked – or at least was described thus in his account – 'like a watchcase or the plate which shields the battery of my radio set'. Another night he fancied returning to Paris 'in a fantastic, high-tech, science-fiction-like machine. I remember the panoramic porthole. Breathtaking speed.'[4] Only a man living at the end of the twentieth century could have such impressions, or, rather, express his delusions in such words.

In the Assyrian dreambook found in Assurbanipal's library, joiners, carpenters, leather-workers, ploughmen, cabinetmakers are mentioned. The lists of trees, plants, vehicles, techniques, jobs, indicate a well-developed urban society with strong craftsmanship skills. Conversely, when Pharaoh, desiring Joseph's opinion (Genesis, 41, 1), relates that in his dream he was standing on a bank of the Nile, and there came up from the river seven cows, sleek and fat, and they 'fed in a meadow', his are the references of a rural economy. The more recent of the two Egyptian dreambooks to have survived, the Papyrus Carlsburg dating from the second century AD, has an entire section dedicated to snakes, not because these had a symbolical meaning but because there were plenty of them on the Nile's banks.

Such examples, sceptics claim, show how eminently social dreams are. Their content is swayed by the dreamer's position in the world and by the context in which he or she is living. The reports are chiefly shaped by how and when they are delivered. Seventeenth-century clergymen, such as William Laud or Ralph Josselin, dreamed of services or of stays in a church. George Fox, the preacher, imagined violent struggles. Attacked, he beat his assailant – all these episodes being symbols of an everlasting battle against evil. Both Ruskin and Katherine Mansfield had encounters with literary figures of their time and talked with them. 'The thoughts or actions of the day', Thomas Browne observed, 'are acted over and echoed in the night. Who can wonder, then, that Chrysostome should dream of St Paul, who daily read his Epistles?' Signs borrowed from the social environment constantly pervade individual vagaries. A vision reported by Graham Greene illustrates the process. The novelist 'saw' two men; one was 'a general in German intelligence', the other Hitler, but 'more human'. Greene had a long chat with Hitler. Oddly enough, he did not realize that his fantasy was a replica of Chaplin's film *The Great Dictator*. In the final sequence, the dictator has been fortuitously arrested; the Jewish barber, who is his double, 'but more human', is mistaken for him and seen from afar strolling with 'a general in German intelligence', who is an honest soldier.

Dreams are about the dreamers, their personal situations, their hopes and their worries. Many in a deteriorating situation, upset by the prospect of a fall in status – countrymen, clerks, secretaries, middle executives, all under a lot of strain – relate dreams filled with images of disintegration and loss. A 30-year-old shop assistant repeatedly fancied she had been sacked and was obliged to go back to her grandparents' farm. In her dream she had changed clothes, was old and dirty, and did not dare look at herself in a mirror. In his dreams a manager of the same age often had trouble with his boss and was also given the sack. He drifted around in a car with his family, not knowing where to go, wondering whether they would accept him on a farm – a scene frequently mentioned in dream accounts since John Ford's film *The Grapes of Wrath*. The roaming dream, the car or coach travel involving an accident, the whole family destroyed, the dreamer left alone, job loss, family as a refuge and a burden, aimless peregrinations seem to be recurrent among the lower-middle class, especially in times of crisis. Nocturnal vagaries offer a simple condensation of diffuse, perennial fears. Conversely, young scientists, professionals, executives, often report dreams of a quiet, unproblematic ascent. They fly, they drive fast cars, go yachting. Is there an engine? A sail? Is it the breeze that propels them? They do not care, nor do they know where they are going, but they enjoy a deep sense of liberty and ease.

Thoreau credited dreams with reflecting our state of mind. He had long been upset by a conflict with a friend who blamed him for a misdeed he had not committed, but after a while he was able to have a dream in which 'justice was at length done me for his suspicions and I received that compensation which I had never obtained in my waking hours. I was unspeakably soothed and rejoiced, ever after I awoke, because in dreams we never deceive ourselves, nor are deceived, and this seemed to have the authority of a final judgement.'[5] Having got over his sorrow, Thoreau managed for himself privately what could not be done overtly with his fellow men.

So, the sceptical postulation goes, dreams translate ordinary human needs and indifferent aspects of life, individual or collective. Most of our information on sleep is gathered by physiologists working in laboratories with artificially awake volunteers, or by doctors who care more for pathological data than for social analysis. Still, researchers cannot blindly rely on materials collected for scientific or medical purposes. We must attempt to listen to the dreams of 'ordinary people' who are not paid to dream or are not following a course of analytical treatment. Instead of scrutinizing a few visions in minute detail we should treat our documents statistically. Psychologists make much of concealments and small tricks that necessarily falsify many an individual account. A larger sample based on familiar interviews made outside of laboratories, the sceptics continue, will reveal extremely simple issues, namely physical impressions, vague feelings and unconnected residues of diurnal activities. A grocer will have a grocer's dreams, a policeman a policeman's . . . A shop assistant dreams that his department supervisor seizes him, packages him, sticks on the package a label that reads 'To be stored' and puts him on a shelf. Such a delusion encapsulates all the beliefs and worries of a sales person and does not go beyond that. The manager is much taller and stronger than his subordinate: he treats the former as that person treats the goods he has not sold. The fear of being made redundant pervades the whole story, which is slightly fantastic but none the less logical and coherent. Is it then unreasonable to assume that dreams clumsily duplicate waking life, and for that reason are not worth lengthy investigations?

Where Sleepers do not Fear to Tread

Although radical and excessive, the sceptical view is valuable. Grand theories are attractive because they illuminate all aspects of their subject and make them perfectly comprehensible. It is therefore good to be faced with the regular intrusion of our personal occupations in dreams. No general system is necessary to comment on these direct, elementary images, artless reflections of humdrum duties. But scepticism is also short-sighted. It does not allow for the creative power of dreams, and disregards the unknown, unpredictable characters and situations that cross our minds at night. Its justified call for research on large dream samples seems to confirm its assertions, but at the same time contradicts them, inasmuch as it detects in dream reports not only personal daily concerns but also general trends made apparent through long periods of time.

Let us study some purely formal aspects of dream accounts. Many, in various periods, state that their vision was taking place at a particular spot. It was here or there, at home, in a street, on the seashore. Dreamers see locations they know – Pharaoh, the banks of the Nile; Ruskin, English landscapes; James Woodforde, a squire's mansion; Perec a shabby Paris flat. Other descriptions are less precise. But most dreamtellers are aware of some sense of space in their experiences. Another familiar feature of dream description is the apprehension of an external presence. Narrators remember finding themselves somewhere with men or women, at times unknown, at others familiar, but unidentified and shadowy. A dream of king Nabonidus quoted in a Babylonian inscription reads: 'in a dream a man stood beside me and said to me . . .'; and later 'in the same dream one attendant appeared to me standing on a chariot'. In *Rhesos,* an anonymous Greek tragedy of the fifth century BC, a coach-driver reports that 'in my dream a figure stood by me'. William Laud and John Wesley 'saw' ill-defined human figures they could not accost. Jung's fancies were full of mysterious, blurred appearances – 'a young man from the country'; 'a piercing whistle that seemed to resound through the whole universe'; 'a huge thing . . . made of skin and naked flesh'; 'an unknown, brown-skinned man, a savage'.

Since they persist throughout centuries, both notions of site and indistinct company suggest that dream accounts share some common features. These may be rhetorical effects produced by the relation itself. We know neither when nor how people began reporting their dreams. Nothing prevents us from supposing that they adopted quite early the conventions of narration still characteristic of most dream accounts, but this would merely be an unprovable guess. We can only say that for more than four millennia, a few themes have regularly been touched on.

Pre-eminent among them is sexuality. The theme is recurrent in dreambooks, medical treatises and scientific debates. To offer a few examples, the Papyrus Carlsburg, the Egyptian dreambook mentioned earlier, has an entire section dedicated to 'The kind of sexual intercourse of which one dreams', while the chapter on sex is the longest in Artemidorius' *Interpretation of Dreams*, and the only part of this work offering developed reflections instead of brisk, straightforward statements. I have to hand a few handouts used to advertise a French dreambook (see opposite). The sleepers are young ladies. The cage has long been a symbol of virginity (to be opened), the rabbit a symbol of female genitalia (Latin: *cuniculus*, from which derives 'cunt', the Spanish *conejo*, the French *con*). Yet, before Freud, the actual importance of sex in dreams was seldom, if ever, systematically scrutinized. Other specialists have criticized his generalizations. For them the erotic drive baffles appraisal all the more that in a dream the same thing can be simultaneously a banal object and a sexual symbol. This may be so. I am unable to decide whether Freud disclosed some hidden truth or whether he was mistaken, though he has provided us with a wealth of new insights. Dreams, before Freud, considered innocent, banal visions are now, rightly or wrongly, labelled sexual dreams and analysed as such.

While helping to enlarge the debate, psychoanalysis has also complicated the issue. Exploring his dreams Freud came to the conclusion that they were distorted representations of repressed infantile wishes. His claim is that in our childhood we were longing for sexual relations with our parents. Society prevented us from fulfilling our desires. Yet far from vanishing, these wishes were stored in our unconscious and emerge at night when our consciousness is dulled. Since they would horrify us, the dreamwork disguises them in acceptable fantasies. At the time of *The Interpretation of*

Dreams, Freud was adamant in his point of view, and the cases he analyzed all seemed to support his theory. Less intransigent at the end of his life, he hinted that it was impossible to give a universally valid description.[6] People had different reactions and distinct ways of dreamtelling, according to social status or to family background.

Although undeveloped by Freud this remark opens new prospects for the reading of dream accounts. Again, I do not attempt to interpret dreams. I attempt only to understand how they are reported. Accounts collected at all times show that a great many people were not, and are still not, disturbed by extravagant sexual fancies. Nor do they feel ashamed by having had, in their dreams, intercourse with their parents, children or relatives. Far from awakening in distress, many observers confess that they tremendously enjoyed what they experienced. St Augustine was upset when he woke after a voluptuous dream. However, he never spoke of leaping to his feet to stop a shockingly pleasant fantasy. Many people do not feel depressed when they recall openly erotic dreams. In Sophocles' *Oedipus Rex*, Oedipus is frightened by a dream in which he marries his mother, but Jocasta cheers him: 'Don't be afraid of this wedding with your mother. In dreams, a man often marries his mother. Those who worry about such mental fantasies feel quite uneasy.' This scene has often been quoted by commentators intent on showing that the Greeks believed in the predictive power of dreams. On the other hand, few stressed Jocasta's reaction to Oedipus' report. Still, it is worth noticing that a fifth-century Greek woman found incestuous dreams perfectly natural.

Ann Faraday candidly tells, 'I had several lovely dreams of my brother making love to me from behind and was very cross to be awakened from them by the alarm clock . . . I feel much more sexually attracted toward my brother since having had my dreams of incest . . . I am no longer surprised at some of my dreams, in which I was sexually assaulted by my mother, who possessed a penis.'[7] Few dreamers are as direct as this, and confessions such as hers often provoke embarrassment when made in public. Three different levels of information should be distinguished: the dream itself, the dreamers' acknowledgement of its sexual nature, and the report delivered by the dreamer. We are not dealing with the first point, since the informant's bias can never be satisfactorily evaluated. Admitting that one has had erotic visions seems relatively easy. St Augustine recognized it, though he never disclosed the content of his fancies. In the 1950s, a physician, Alfred Kinsey, anxious to analyze the sexual behaviour of Americans, sent questionnaires to more than 10.000 men and women. As they were not asked to give their name, most filled in the forms willingly. Their answers proved the frequency of blatantly erotic dreams, often accompanied by orgasm. Yet no precise details were solicited. Kinsey's figures and statistics provide an interesting but limited clue: voluptuous dreams are common for both sexes.

Describing them, however, is another matter. According to their character, individuals will conceal erotic visions if they feel ashamed, confess them reluctantly or embellish them. Jung's accounts reach a level of sublimation where any hint at sexuality would sound shocking. William Laud, who recorded his dreams for twenty years, or Coleridge, never noted an erotic one. Byron did not go further than whispering 'If I sin in my dream . . .'. Ruskin's ingenuous description of a vision in which 'there was a nice sober girl whom I took a great fancy to, but I forget how it went on' (6 December 1869) would surely cause a psychoanalyst to smile. While avoiding precise details, Schnitzler did not hide his dreams' sexual character. One night (10 August 1928), he dreamed of being in a hotel room with a friend; she behaved tenderly, and, although bound to leave, stayed with him. Another night (19 June 1928), he fancied a theatre, where he met 'on the left, against the wings, a naked slave', whom he contemplated with interest; 'after she had said something the slave left in a fur coat.' Telling overtly sexual dreams is either prohibited or encouraged by the cultural context. In some periods the topic has been almost taboo. How should we interpret the relative silence of accounts in those periods, for instance during the nineteenth century? What did people censor: their dreams or their reports? At other times, talking sex is fashionable. Do public debates on the subject induce people to have nocturnal sexual fancies or to deliver more precise accounts? And what about the periods when sex, while still an essential aspect of life, is not a topic of conversation? A cursory vision of history induces us to consider the Victorian era as one of strong social pressure, where openly erotic scenes or images could not appear in dreams, whereas free rein would be given to erotic fantasies in the contemporary world. Have we significant evidence to confirm or refute this opinion?

Many today see erotic symbols in elongated or circular objects, and interpret seemingly indifferent situations as potentially sexual. Dream reports appear freer than before, but careful study reveals a rather complicated situation. A young lady involved in an university experiment proved reluctant one morning to relate what she had fancied. Her fellow students urged her to talk. Eventually she made up her mind:

'Well, you know, it was absurd. It was a room, maybe a flat. I was there with students, all boys. Then there was a letter for one of the boys. I had to carry it. He was in the bathroom, having a shower. He went out dripping with water, all naked, and he was there, in front of me, reading the letter and I was looking at him, like that and . . . nothing, it was absolutely meaningless.'

In such case the young lady's reaction, her initial hesitation, her embarrassment, point toward a sexual reading of the dream. A different account given immediately with a laugh or an obvious lack of personal concern would make the dream unimportant and deprived of connotation. Why did the girl flush? Because she felt excited while having her vision? Or because being a psychology student she was aware of Freudian theory, and retrospectively attributed to her fantasies a signification they did not necessarily have?

On the other hand, it seems that the popularization of the basic ideas of psychoanalysis has deeply influenced dream accounts. Just take a look at Perec's confidences. They sound like a triumphal crow rather than an objective report, and few novelists, if any, would have dared publish such material in the nineteenth century:

'In this dream I am lying on a bed with a woman whom I eventually identify (deeply moved and stunned, as if I had long waited for that impossible meeting) as C. We are both enthralled by an intense pleasure . . . I am lying on my back. C. impales herself on me, but she moves and I go out of her. She starts lamenting what has happened, which excites me. She kneels, and, leaning behind her, I penetrate her again. Copulating, we start creeping over the fitted carpet.'[8]

There is, in Perec's tale, a narrative coherence generally lacking in patchy, telegraphic dream accounts. But its most striking feature is the crude description of sexual intercourse. Shall we say that decisive changes in everyday morality allow contemporary writers to report fantasies previously censored? Or is it merely a question of style, the same stories being told less overtly in past times? A Hittite collection of dreams experienced by members of royal families considers dreams where a queen has been bothered by husky men.[9] In other words, this lady could report whatever she had dreamed during the night, provided she transferred the responsibility to male aggressors. In Jerusalem, before the destruction of the Temple by the Romans, the high priest could not act according to his sacred functions after a nocturnal pollution. Therefore, any time a relative substituted for him, the whole community was indirectly informed of his recent dreams. His flock quietly commented: 'he seems in a dream to have had intercourse with a woman'.[10]

In the literature of pre-capitalist communities we find numerous examples of overt sexual intercourse or reports using symbols readily identified by the dreamers as representations of sexual relationships. What must be considered is the important role played by religious factors in these accounts. In the case of the Jewish high priest, this is obvious, but even in the Hittite document a religious compensation was stipulated to erase the insult to the queen. The erotic dream was taken in by the nets of social organization; the sexual and the sacred were closely associated, at least in the report of dreams. According to investigations made at the beginning of the twentieth century, the Mahori of the southwest Pacific attached much importance to their sexual delusions. Dreaming of intercourse with a person other than one's usual partner implied a particular connection with that person. In a population where love relationships were treated openly and without reserve, sexual dreams had a special status. As they were different from ordinary affairs, they entailed a courtship between those involved in the dream. When the research was carried out, the ritual was a trace of a period when sexual fancies concerned the whole society. In such cases, making one's dreams known to the community seemed perfectly normal. On the other hand, in modern, industrial or post-industrial societies, the group is not interested in private confessions: individuals freely decide to conceal or disclose their privacy.

Shall we say that accounts of erotic visions are regulated by cultural traditions and social norms? Dreambooks prevent us from being content with an obvious but rather banal conclusion. These volumes are strongly influenced by the historical context. For instance, in rural communities like ancient Egypt,[11] dreaming of mating with a cow was considered a commonplace delusion – generally interpreted as a good sign because it meant scattering one's semen – while contemporary, urban societies are wholly unfamiliar with this kind of dream. However, throughout history, manuals dealing with dreams are filled with the same erotic fancies. The oldest Assyrian dreambook – factual, precise and sober – offers reflections about the penis, its shape, its use, and mentions several sexual relationships, such as sleeping with a woman, kissing her lips, touching her breasts. The matter-of-fact tone is as neutral in this paragraph as in the sections devoted to agricultural activities or trade. In antiquity, sodomy and incest were commonplaces of divination books, as they were when Freud was studying dreams, and they are still so today. I have mentioned the importance of Artemidorius' volume and its effect on most later treatises. The Greek soothsayer was extraordinarily meticulous. However, in his strange evocations there was neither moralism nor salaciousness. Our post-Freudian heritage could induce us to believe he reproved visions where a son turned his mother around in order to make love to her from behind (I, 78) or while standing up (I, 79). In fact, he merely thought that such positions, signalling haste or the lack of a bed to lie on, foretold destitution or restrictions. The acts were not important: attention had to be focused on circumstances. Seen in that light, perversions were auspicious inasmuch as they were comfortable.

Almost all the cases cited here are from a male point of view. Today, dreambooks for sale in supermarkets are bought equally by women and men. Was there a totally different clientele in ancient times? Or was it assumed that women had no sexual dreams? However rare, in ancient manuals we do find instances of female erotic visions. We have already noted one queen's, mentioned in a Hittite document. Artemidorius tells the story of a woman who had sexual relations with her own child, but insists that it was 'because of an unlucky incident, and unwittingly'. Other dreambooks cite Io's dream in Aeschylus' *Prometheus Bound* (c. 650 BC). Titillated by desire, the young lady hears a voice saying: 'Zeus is eager to enjoy with you Aphrodite's pleasures . . . Young lady, don't spurn Zeus' bed, go to Lerne's meadow, land of pasture, let Zeus' ardour find appeasement after so many longings' (lines 645–53). In these texts women are passive, their sexual drives are inflamed by bold men or through some mishap. We may suppose that interpretation manuals were understood 'backwards' by women, 'making love to one's mother' becoming, for instance, in the reader's mind, 'being assaulted by one's son'.

Intepretation books have always taken dreams as signs. Since dream content is of little importance to them, they have used recurrent themes to help people cope with confusing delusions. The cold listing of various erotic performances reduced the emotional strain possibly associated with voluptuous images and made these impressions perfectly innocuous. Highbrows rightly tax these volumes as simplistic. But dream manuals were not concerned with establishing in the sleepers a better comprehension of their subjective problems; they attempted to catalogue normal, predictable occurrences. They showed that any sexual behaviour could be visualized in sleep. Their continuity throughout the centuries offers another enigma. Undoubtedly, dream accounts follow definite patterns and are ruled by the unspoken models typical of an epoch: Ruskin would never have told a voluptuous dream in the manner that Perec did, and, vice-versa, Perec did not need Ruskin's circumlocutions. Yet the same practices, the same experiences, have been repeatedly memorized and mentioned in dreambooks by successive generations.

'Just as a Snake Casts Off its Old Skin'

Dream reports interweave common human needs, local habits, cultural traditions and ways of using language. Where food, clothes, manners, money, religion or hierarchies are involved, conventions prevail. Historians can learn a great deal about an epoch by studying its dreams. It is an excellent way of discovering the hopes and fears of those that lived through it. It is difficult, for instance, to know what ordinary people thought during troubled times, but dream accounts are likely to betray their deepest feelings. It is revealing to find wounds or corporeal injuries occurring in dreams experienced in the 1640s during the English Civil Wars. Fascinating though this is, I chose sexuality as our starting-point because it is simple and universal in its aims, limited in its practices, limitless in its verbal expressions.

Death and what goes with it – violence, anxiety, revolt – is another merging point between the general human condition, local and national customs, historical contexts and language. 'Slumber, the sister of death', Byron wrote. All sleepers can experiment the strange sensation of being dead and witnessing their own corpse – an impression rarely felt in a waking state, except by seriously psychotic people. Artemidorius expressed this uncanny feeling perfectly when he cited a man who dreamed that 'he slipped out of his flesh just as a snake casts off its old skin'. It is more than undressing. Skin, flesh, external form have been left behind, and yet the individual remains what he or she was previously. The opening paragraph of Nerval's *Aurélia* attempts to lure the reader into the 'invisible world' of another life. 'The first instants of sleep are an image of death': we feel sunk in a misty lethargy, so that 'we are unable to decide the precise moment when the *self*, in some other form, continues the work of existence'; it is now in the state and place of Limbo, where bodyless souls exist.

A letter by a North African Muslim in the tenth century exemplifies this astonishing awareness. In his dream, after he died, his soul was 'given back' to him – he still existed, but he was totally hollow. It was only after his soul had been returned to him that the hole was filled. The man was then able to observe:

> '*I perceived all that people were doing to me: the washing of my body, the shroud, prayers. When they had put me in the ground someone called me, shouting to me to recite. My tongue recited the Sura 36. Two angels arrived. One said to the other: "Examine him" – "Don't you hear him reciting the heart of the Koran?", replied the other; and they went off without further interrogation.*'[12]

Estrangement from one own's body seen from without, like a familiar but exterior object, is repeatedly evoked in dream accounts. We saw in previous chapters Perec and Freud quietly witnessing their evisceration. Ruskin had once 'a quite formidably clear dream of taking a large front tooth out, with part of the jaw, and looking to see how much defigured I was'. Others report they dreamed of dissecting themselves or having their bowels taken out, as if it were necessary to tear up the imprisoned soul.

Mental and physical condition, state of mind, age, historical circumstances – all weigh heavily on the sleeper's impressions. Dreamers looking at their corpse put into a coffin may be fearing suffocation if, at that moment, they have trouble breathing. At times the encounter with one's alienated body is painful and turns into a nightmare: the sleeper attempts to resist the destructive forces or to rebuild his or her self. In the worst periods of his life, Coleridge dreamed of having parts of his body pulled out. He did his best to take them back, awoke screaming, and realized that these body parts were hurting him. Such connections reveal individual behaviours and reactions, but fail to explain why this stunning personality split is so frequent in sleep.

Divided into separated entities – body and spirit, dreamers evade their daily world; their visions unfold outside the accepted order and challenge it, making them free to kill. In their dreams peaceable individuals may turn into murderers. Kafka, whose dreams included injuries made to his person, had astonishingly brutal delusions. He relates in his *Diaries*[13] how one night he imagined the capture of a tall naked man. With his friends he wanted to stab a knife into the prisoner, but they found no knife. Nearby was an oven. They carried the man to it, put one of his feet on the fire until it smoked, pulled it back and then returned it to the fire. Ruskin's sleep was filled with cruel scenes in which he was a witness, not an actor. Jung's visions led generally to a highly moral, heart-warming conclusion. Yet he once dreamed of carefully laying an ambush and killing a defenceless Siegfried, the famous hero of the *Niebelungenlied*.[14]

Death and violence, wounds, aggression are closely associated in dreams. Some dreamers are upset by their visions: Kafka awoke from his torture episode 'in cold sweat with my teeth chattering'; Jung awoke with 'an unbearable feeling of guilt'. Even though not all were upset, many people have been astonished by the brutal, disturbing content of their dreams. In the ancient world it was generally accepted that upsetting dreams announced physiological disorders, and the soothsayers were all too ready to establish simple connections. According to them, someone who saw sanguinary images received a warning that harm was about to happen. Today, while pretending to be scientific and sceptical, many stick to the older view. But death dreams or violent visions are very common; few people actually die following the sight in a dream of their corpse. Even so, in one letter (16 October 1797) Coleridge reported how his father was visited, during his sleep, by 'Death as he is commonly painted' and died a few days later. Exhausted after a long journey, Coleridge's father appears to have suffered a premonition shortly before succumbing to a heart attack.

Artemidorius and his successors extensively exploited these synchronisms. More cautious contemporary dream manuals[15] do not mention 'prophetic visions' but claim that dreams are likely to represent things about to happen, especially when they concern predictable events. According to these books, secret worries or desires we forget in our conscious mind, illnesses we do not wish to acknowledge, nevertheless condition our dreams until finally we wake up to a full awareness of our problems. Contrasting an old with a modern conception of dreams would therefore be misleading, not only because many still believe in the premonitory power of dreams but also because in the past some people were aware of the informative power of dreams. Over three centuries ago, Thomas Browne noted: 'However dreams may be fallacious concerning outward events, yet may they be truly significant at home, whereby we may more sensibly understand ourselves.'

Browne added: 'Many dreams are made out from the signature of their subjects'; we generate them, they are part of our life and are capable not only of anticipating, but of making our future. St Augustine had already been confronted with the problem, and his formulations are worth particular attention. As a true believer he respected what may have been God's messages. Yet he could not but perceive an obvious interference on the part of the dreamer due to personal concerns. At the time he was still an atheist, his mother, Monica, had a dream. She was standing on a piece of wood, feeling great sorrow because of her son's behaviour. A beautiful young man approached her. He said 'that where she was, there I was also', and Monica suddenly saw her son beside her on the piece of wood. Previously, she had turned her son out of the house. Convinced that God had sent her his instructions, she allowed Augustine to come home. Mother and son argued about the meaning of the dream. Against his scepticism she maintained that she could easily discern the difference between God's revelations and her own fantasies. Such irrepressible conviction made a great impression on Augustine. Monica went on asking God for advice about Augustine's future, but she received no answer. The mystical vision had been a unique event. Augustine soon left Africa, and many years passed before his conversion.

This episode in the *Confessions* (III, 11 and VI, 13) reveals Augustine's embarrassment. He did not hide the fact that after her vision, Monica 'saw some fantastic things' clearly related to her current concerns, chiefly to her preoccupation with her son, and lost confidence in her dreams. Prudently

Augustine called God to witness: 'You heard her. I mean, could her dream be sent from any other place?' But he was disconcerted by the (all too predictable?) consequences of the dream: it had obviously modified Monica's mood, brought together mother and son, eventually resulted in Augustine's change of mind.

Augustine did not go so far as to see in the dream an event Monica wished to happen. While his predecessors could not, or did not want to, go too far, Jung, starting from the same premises, arrived at an unambiguous conclusion. If dreams sometimes hint at veiled difficulties or concern infantile wishes, they more often disclose neglected future prospects. A few examples[16] allowed him to show how, in given circumstances, a dream had foretold what would occur. One of his patients, a mountain climber, often dreamed of stepping off the summit of a high mountain into empty space. Indeed, one day, this is exactly what he did. His dreams were directed toward the future, not toward the past. Time and again he rehearsed the scene in his sleep, and became so obsessed by the event that finally he performed it in the open air.

Dream Themes / Dream Reports

Seen in such a light, dream content is perfectly comprehensible provided the sleeper is ready to receive its message. Three millennia ago the Babylonian king Nabonidus reported a vision that frightened him until a reassuring explanation was found in the dream itself.[17] Dreams, Thomas Browne affirmed, carry 'their interpretation in their fundamental sense'; those who understand 'upon what natural fundamental' they are based 'hold a ready way to read the characters of Morpheus'. Jung found it useless to devise a systematic reading method. In his view, patients often needed guidance toward a personal interpretation, but inasmuch as dreams generally disclose themselves, curiosity and discernment are sufficient.

When the awaking sleeper does not immediately grasp the significance of a vision, a dream report is likely to illuminate this meaning. According to Jungians, a dream report is, in itself, an interpretation, and tells the dreamer the meaning of the dream. A secretary wrote:

> I've started dreaming about my boss. The dreams are vivid and filled with emotional longing and sexual desire, although I have never felt anything towards him in real life. In fact, a lot of the time he drives me mad. He is elusive and a complete control freak. Recently, though, the dreams have become so powerful and disturbing they are starting to affect my relationship with my husband. They stay in my head all day and I feel as though I am keeping a secret from him.

This insightful, perceptive account provides an exegesis of its writer's dreams and offers a diagnosis concerning its future consequences. But in order to remove her doubts and gain direct access to her problem, the woman has been obliged to emphasize one aspect of her fantasies. A well-trained soothsayer, Artemidorius argued (III, 66), must find dreams' central ideas, and dreambooks all reduce dreams to one topic. There is a wide gap between an accurate dream report and the selection of one theme, however important it looks. The letter cited above seems perfectly clear. Yet it was written as a request for advice. Why do people who clearly know what is at stake require an external opinion? The reason is that they hesitate to take into account the details of their dreams or to grasp their essence. If they go directly to what they regard as crucial, they oversimplify. If they take into consideration the dreams' complexities, they are lost. Sleepers often call for an exegesis because, in their view, only dream inter-preters can ease their anxiety.

CHAPTER FIVE

The Power of Dream Interpreters

Reporting a dream to oneself or to another is the best way to organize vague perceptions and to give them some consistency. The telling itself illuminates the meaning of the dream for the dreamer. No one knows to what extent the account reflects or betrays the contents of the dream. However, if the dream can be communicated, it is no longer the sleeper's. André Breton urged the Surrealists to publicize their dreams. Publication, he assumed, would allow them to master their dreams and prevent their internal censors from blurring them. Relate to a friend what you have dreamed as soon after as possible, Breton said. So, later, if your memory tricks you, someone can remind you of your initial version. Coleridge, Wordsworth and members of their group circulated their dreams, not in order to discover an explanation but to translate them into words. Absurd or mysterious dreams look less worrying once they have been reported or written down; clear accounts give them a more conventional aspect. Once Lewis Carroll's Alice has told her sister her 'strange adventures', everything seems to return to normal and the family can enjoy afternoon tea.

The dreamer is the only person able to describe her or his dreams and able to detect the wishes or fears they may conceal. This is what Freud and Jung had in mind when they decided to scrutinize their own dreams. Jung reported some of his experiences to Freud, but he never trusted his mentor's explanations. Both refused to ask for an external opinion and instead performed what they called *self analysis*. Yet they spent most of their professional lives listening to other people, describing their dreams and attempting to interpret them. Moreover, they instructed their disciples in how to read their patients' dreams.

There is something odd in our attitude toward dreams. They are *private* perceptions. Communicating them is difficult; it is never fully satisfying. But we are not always self-confident enough to sort out their meaning, and often prefer to ask a friend for an opinion. Some choose professional exegetes. What prompts people to put their trust in an individual they hardly know? What do they hope for? What influence do they grant to the exegete? Are diviners, soothsayers, psychoanalysts radically different as specialists? Or do they share common characteristics? This is the question explored below.

A Study in Violet

An Italian psychoanalyst working in the United States once told me about one of his cures. His client was a widow. Born in New York of an Italian family, she lived with her son, who, having been badly injured in a car crash, was returned to his mother's home, an invalid for life. The widow, suffering from clinical depression, sought help from my friend. As she was beginning to recover, her dreams were filled with violet clothes, violet furniture, violet walls . . . Everything was violet. She felt ill at ease. There was nothing painful in the dreams, but since violet was the colour of mourning she thought that, unconsciously, she was somehow burying her son. She complained more about the mysterious character of her dreams than about the impression they made on her. Her analyst reported the case to other Italians, who reminded him of a Mediterranean tradition. In rural Italy, at the beginning of the twentieth century, middle-class widows continued to wear black for some time after a husband's death before choosing violet, a colour with a precise meaning: these women would not marry again, but for them bereavement was over. Violet was often called the 'half-mourning' colour. My friend informed his client, but left her to decide whether she stuck to her pessimistic interpretation or whether violet, far from hinting at her son's death, meant she had accepted her sad, difficult situation in the way Italian widows accepted their own condition. Shortly after, the widow ended her analysis.

This story raises important problems. First there is the patient's attitude. Her dreams themselves were not repetitive. But she blocked attempts to investigate her other dreams and fixed only on one theme. She was set on one colour, and decided it was a message she was sending to herself. Violet, she acknowledged, was not threatening. Quite the opposite – it looked soothing. And yet she fixed on an unpleasant interpretation, while urging the analyst to give his opinion. Whatever the meaning she finally chose (and she did not tell her analyst), she obtained an answer, one different from her own, to the riddle she had created out of her nocturnal impressions. The dreams, or rather an aspect selected by the patient, made her clinically depressed. Here, the analyst had his part to play, though he was never to discover whether his words were heeded.

Did not the woman feel uneasy because at the back of her mind she was aware of the 'half mourning' tradition but could not remember it? Or did she merely want the analyst to pay attention to her distress, without hoping for any precise interpretation? My friend was all the more puzzled since he had taken the recurrent colour seriously and tried hard to understand its significance. As he later realized, he had not told his Italians friends this story by chance; his steps after he had heard the dream account had been oriented by what he knew about his patient. The report about violet, he saw afterwards, had been a watershed in the cure. Though a dedicated Freudian he did not dare give the woman a clear-cut interpretation. Did he not attempt to offer clues for a reading because he guessed that the woman might soon leave him, and considered it his duty to advise her on what she ought to think?

What the story makes clear is the complex exchange dreams can generate. Our woman needed to be heard by another person, but maybe that was all. Was there a specific meaning in the return of the colour? Was it not merely a sign? Sleepers report their visions, but they do not, and probably cannot, tell what they want their interlocutor to do. Interpreters have to adopt a position with regard to the account (will they consider all its intricacies or look for its leading idea?) and with regard to their client's expectations. Theirs would be a risky situation were it not for the fact that all societies organize their members' social function. The range of roles attributed to dream exegetes is far from unlimited; the strategies analysts adopt and the social benefits they obtain from their work are reducible to a few, simple patterns.

Diviners

Ancient societies despised dream interpreters. In Mesopotamia their function was generally consigned to women. But the diviners, mediators between deities and mankind, belonged to a different, much revered category. Entrusted with questioning the gods and deciphering their enigmatic answers, they looked at various signs and delivered factual, practical answers. The Greeks and Romans seem to have had little regard for nocturnal revelations. When the plague was raging in their camp, preventing them from sailing towards Troy (*Iliad*, I, 62), Achilles proposed to consult a prophet, a priest even, and for want of something better, a dream exegete. Talking about those who deciphered the divine instructions in sanctuaries,

Plato (*Timaeus*, 72) said: 'They, are named "diviners" by people who do not understand that they are not diviners but merely translators of enigmatic voices and apparitions. "Interpreters of divine revelations" should be their true name.' King Astyages had a vision he could not understand and turned to 'those of the Magi who interpret dreams', but Herodotus, who reported the fact (I, 107), did not omit to signal he was a Medean, not a Greek. 'Of divination by dreams, each of us is perforce his own instrument', provided we are open minded, patient and attentive, Synesius of Cyrene contended. 'Many books have been collected' by dream interpreters, he added, but 'for my part I laugh at these books and think them of little use': dream divination is a hopeless business, since all men are different.

We must not be misled by such apparent unanimity. Literature is often at variance with people's strongest beliefs, and this is especially true where dreams are concerned. Dreambooks loom large among the oldest writings, they have been transmitted and copied throughout generations because they fall in with recurring problems. Even kings, princes and generals indulged in questioning dreams when they were in a quandary. According to a Sumerian text of Assurbanipal's epoch, dreams by priests and even dreams by anonymous individuals were reported to the king at a time when he was challenged by military attacks by his enemies. These visions announcing the miserable death of Assurbanipal's foes and granting the king the goddess Ishtar's help were welcome, and were thought worth recording in an official document. Achilles scorned dreamtellers, but was resigned to consulting them. Later, in the Roman period, Flavius Josephus mentioned ironically the case of a high Roman dignitary, Archealus, governor of Judaea, who, being upset by a dream he could not understand, 'sent for the soothsayers'.[1] The long-lasting fortune of all kind of exegesis shows how anxious dreamers have always sought reassurances.

Philosophers intent on eliminating what they considered false knowledge never prevented people from consulting a soothsayer, but they succeeded in arousing suspicion against these professionals. In a

Mediterranean world badly disposed towards dream-reading and prone to regard it as a second-rate, ill-founded activity, Israel was an exception. Jacob's son, Joseph, has sometimes been called the founding father in a series of exegetes who have links through to modern psychoanalysts. He was not the first dream interpreter, for many Mesopotamians had preceded him. But, more than a mere soothsayer, he was a diviner, a man who, not content with clarifying puzzling dreams, was able, thanks to divine blessing, to understand and communicate God's message. Of course Joseph, as well as Daniel, the other biblical diviner, are mythical figures. They manifest in a picturesque, lively manner the original vision of dream and dream-reading conveyed by the Bible.

The biblical God had previously taken advantage of sleep to help or to inform Joseph's ancestors, first Abraham (Genesis, 20, 3–6) and then Jacob. In one dream (Genesis, 28, 13) he had told Jacob: 'I *am* the Lord God of Abraham thy father, and the God of Isaac: the land whereon thou liest, to thee will I give it, and to thy seed.' Receiving divine advice was therefore a tradition in Hebrew culture, and this was sufficient to distinguish a banal, human dream-reading from divination. Joseph did not cease to stress God's initiative. Sent to jail with a couple of Pharaoh's officials, he heard them complain about incomprehensible dreams and said: 'Does not interpretation belong to God?' Summoned to Pharaoh (Genesis, 41, 14), he reacted immediately when the Pharaoh told him 'I have heard say of thee, *that* thou canst understand a dream to interpret it.' Joseph protested: '*It is not* in me: God shall give Pharaoh an answer of peace.' Then, after having explained the dream (the seven years of plenty and the seven of famine), Joseph insisted: 'God hath shewed Pharaoh what he *is* about to do' (Genesis, 41, 25). Similarly, Daniel, invited to reassure king Nebuchadnezzar, whose mind was troubled by a vision, warned him that it was God who 'maketh known to the king Nebuchadnezzar what shall be in the latter days' (Daniel, 2, 28).

Polyteists know neither which god will manifest nor which medium will be used. In their mental world, animals' entrails, birds in flight, thunder, dreams, may or not be significant. The deity is even likely to cheat. So Zeus, in conflict with other gods about the expedition against Troy, sends Agamemnon 'a deceitful dream' (*Iliad*, II, 6) claiming fraudulently that he has convinced all the gods to support his plans. The multiplicity of divine beings gave full scope to the ingeniousness of soothsayers. Monotheism is not allowed the same freedom of interpretation: a unique God can neither send ambiguous messages nor leave exegetes to decide which channel he prefers; his words must be comprehensible and his means of communication easily identifiable. The dilemma was clearly expressed by God himself in the Fourth Book of Moses, Numbers (12, 6-8): 'If there be a prophet among you, *I* the Lord will make myself known unto him in a vision, *and* will speak unto him in a dream.' As a consequence divine communication through dreams is omnipresent in the Bible. During the night God speaks with Solomon (I Kings, 3, 10–15), instructs Gideon how to win the Medianites (Leviticus, 7, 13–14), and withdraws from Saul so that he complains 'God is departed from me, and answereth me no more, neither by prophets, nor by dreams' (I Samuel, 28, 15). Visions, Job recalls, are orders, promises and warnings from God 'In a dream, in a vision of the night, when deep sleep falleth upon men' (Job, 33, 15). God's faithful had a direct contact with him. A passage of Joel (2, 28) announces that, one day, the Lord's spirit will suffuse all mankind, so that everybody will be in touch with him through dreams or visions. Meanwhile, diviners had a role to play: they were put in charge to enlighten those who were not yet elects.

Joseph and Daniel gained wealth and influence because of their skill. In a culture in which dream interpreters were greatly honoured, it was tempting to transform one's dreams into divine manifestations. Admonitions against false diviners are common in the Bible.

> If there arise among you a prophet, or a dreamer of dreams, and
> giveth thee a sign or a wonder,

And the sign or the wonder come to pass, whereof he spake unto thee, saying, Let us go after other gods, which thou hast not known, and let us serve them;

Thou shalt not hearken unto the words of that prophet, or that dreamer of dreams . . . (Deuteronomy, 13, 1–3)

God also threatened to send empty visions full of daily concerns but deprived of mystical significance (Ecclesiastes, 5, 6). Jeremiah's imprecations (23, and 29), however obscure they are, give the impression that many Hebrews had recourse to soothsayers for mundane problems, and that the interpreters they consulted were women – while, of course, diviners were all men.

Although the Bible was the cornerstone of monotheist religions, neither Christianity nor Islam endorsed dream divination. The diviner, empowered to make known God's will and views about human affairs, disappeared during the first millennium after Christ. There were still legions of dream interpreters, but their function was fairly different from Joseph's or Daniel's. Up to now historians have been unable to account for this transformation.

Divination was widely current in the first centuries of Christianity. It was forbidden by the Ancyra Council in 314, but prohibitions often show the social importance of a practice (otherwise such condemnations would be worthless). The punishment was very mild, probably because the Council did not dare challenge the diviners, whose influence was still considerable. Mystical visions served religious propaganda; miraculous dreams were circulated to prove the truth of Jesus' teaching. Preachers never fail to relate how, during sleep, the emperor Constantine had been promised victory if he used the sign of the Cross on his standard, nor how, having complied, he won and was converted to Christianity. Less impressive though it is, the centurion Martin's story was also widely circulated. Having given half his cloak to a beggar, Martin was complimented by Christ at night and wished to be baptized.

Yet little by little, dreams became more stereotypal. Christ, an angel or a saint urged dreamers to behave properly, at times threatening them with Hell. The most striking feature of these delusions was their purely individual character: Heaven addressed the faithful about private concerns or about problems regarding another individual. Personal communication between God and an individual man is recorded in the Bible, but this was less important than general messages aimed at the whole people. On the other hand, the nine celestial dreams reported in Matthew and in the Acts of the Apostles were individual, factual, of limited consequences; they were merely orders to go or not go to a given place. It comes as no surprise that Constantine's, Martin's and many others' dreams were timely, personal instructions.

Heavenly revelation did not cease in the Middle Ages, but it was no longer disclosed at night and took another form. Let us compare two experiences. Guibert of Nogent's autobiography, written *c.* 1100, records banal dreams announcing retribution or punishment. Half a century later, Hildegarde of Bingen's dreams were extraordinary poems or meditations full of dazzling images and prophetic sentences. But Hildegarde did not sleep. Wide awake, conscious, alert to bodily sensations, she saw celestial emissaries and registered their words. Hers were the beginning of a series of encounters with God and his go-between, to be continued with Joan of Arc and others, and, more recently, with those who have witnessed the Lourdes and Fatima apparitions. The figures in such visions did not tackle personal concerns; they delivered Joan of Arc instructions, and later revealed to young French or Portuguese shepherds truths to be widely communicated for the spiritual education of all faithful souls.

The decline of dream divination did not take place at a specific time; it is impossible to date it. In the same way we must avoid seemingly obvious correlations. If divination faded in the Muslim world while it was also vanishing in Europe, the relation between these contemporary facts is far from clear. Dream-readers had a clientele, but were disdained in pre-Islamic Arabia as in many other parts of the Middle East. According to the Koran (21, 5) Muhammad's opponents in Mecca accused him of trickery and called his preaching 'a mass of bad dreams, a blasphemy, a poet's work'. The Prophet refuted the allegations concerning blasphemy and poetry, but not what his opponents said about dreams (idem, 41–2). If he never introduced himself as a diviner, he was an interpreter of heavenly inspired dreams or diurnal visions. Nocturnal revelation played a significant part in his life. A dream determined him to attack the powerful city of Mecca, to restore pilgrimages to that city, and finally to gain possession of it. He urged his followers to report their dreams, the Arab historian Ibn Khaldun relates, because these might explain how to accelerate the diffusion of Islam. More important, he was asleep when divine revelation first reached him. The archangel Gabriel ordered him to read God's message, and, though illiterate, he was able to decipher it (Koran, 97, 2). Later, he received at night part of the heavenly announcement. His nocturnal communication with the Almighty, his teaching of supranatural truth announced during sleep, his reading of his own and others' dreams, all are typical experiences of biblical diviners.

Dreams were one of God's means to talk to his people, an aspect of prophecy. For Islam, Muhammad was God's last messenger: no diviner could take his office. Yet the Prophet did not abolish dream interpretation; he was content to limit it to a small group of ill-considered, poor Arabs. The practice continued after his death, but slowly took a different turn. Rich Muslims hired interpreters able to understand God's advice, but also to find useful information about their future in nocturnal images; even ancient dreambooks, mostly of Greek origin, were translated and adapted to Islamic precepts. A new custom, the search for the best choice, developed. Longing for divine inspiration, pious Muslims recited a prayer before going to bed, hoping that God would favour them with an illuminating vision.

Distrust of divination had common aspects in Christianity and Islam. Theologians wondered how it was possible to distinguish divine

from ordinary or misleading dreams. Demons, the Koran (6, 223) said, know how to lure humans into sin by showing them at night tantalizing pictures. In a highly sophisticated way, Hildegarde of Bingen expressed the same worry. Emotions felt during the day, she noted, are reworked during sleep, giving rise to new thoughts. It is easy for the Devil, who knows what has happened, to take a hand and introduce temptation or false ideas in dreams. Both religions emphasized his dark personality and function. An evil but weak spirit in the Bible, he became then a fearsome fiend. Christianity and Islam dwelt on the dirty aspects of dreams, sex, gluttony, covetousness, violence – all manipulated by Satan. Such credence was still spread among religious circles in the eighteenth century. Goya's *Caprichos* made fun of it by showing demons, witches and harpies who *soplan,* that is to say blow dangerous, obscene images into sleeping monks' minds (see opposite). Implicit in Goya's prints was the idea that frustrated monks had lascivious dreams. For resisting the nocturnal eruption of our worse instincts, the best weapons, many thought, were wakefulness and prayer. A few historians go so far as to maintain that during the Middle Ages there was a collective censorship on dreams. But is that enough to explain the decline of dream divination?

Professionals

Divination was only one aspect of dream interpretation; other forms of exegesis can be traced to remote antiquity. To begin with, the diviners' skill was not limited to transmitting heavenly instructions, for they were able to interpret human dreams too. Joseph told Pharaoh's chamberlains what their delusions meant. Flavius Josephus did his comrades in arms the same service. Comments by Flavius Josephus and other experts, as well as those found in ancient and modern dreambooks, inform us about interpreters' basic techniques. It comes as a surprise to see how many categories of dreams are listed in the text-books. Their writers have to anticipate myriads of hypothetical occurrences; many are very peculiar, and probably of no use to the great majority. We cannot but be impressed by the sophistication and meticulousness involved in the entries' choice. There were and still are lazy scribblers content with copying out former works, but, when taken seriously, dream exegesis is not simply a matter of cataloguing questions and answers, it is a demanding occupation.

Yet many feel disappointed by the advice found in their dreambooks because dreams baffle simple, unambiguous categories. Take this short example:

> 'I am in a car (in the front? in the back?). There are three people in the front. My son is driving. He looks at those seated beside him instead of looking at the road, the car falls into a river. I know, it is a dream, it is not true, I can change it, I ask my son to be careful, the car does not slide sideways. My mother tells me that old Charlotte has been murdered. Her husband thinks it is a political murder, she had disclosed a secret, but the police say an inquiry would be useless. Oddly enough, my mother and Charlotte's husband died a long time ago, whereas Charlotte is still alive.'

Dreambooks deal with lack of attention, road casualties, the death of a son, mysterious murders. Some go so far as to mention visions dreamed as pure visions. But what is lacking is the relationship between these various entries. There are in the above dream two deaths immediately denied and an unmotivated jump from one story to another. However elaborated, manuals cannot consider such issues: they describe minutely numerous particulars but do not look for general frames of inference likely to bridge details to a general structure that will encompass everything.

Though inadequate, dreambooks sell very well. Buyers may hope against hope. But there is another explanation for a seemingly irrational purchase. Dreamers are tempted to reduce the vast number of significant images enclosed in their delusions to the limited series of events corresponding to their present worries or expectations. Coincidences are easily found between incidents happening in a dream and deep, sometimes half-hidden, concerns. Dreams often attract our attention to unpleasant thoughts that we would prefer to forget. Parents uneasy about their travelling child would focus on the car crash if they had the dream reported above, while the elderly would be alarmed by the murder of an old lady.

One reason why we remember our dreams, and attempt either to report them integrally or to emphasize a particular aspect, is our own anxiety. Some dreams are perfectly clear, but do not seem to relate to the sleeper's activities. The cows I saw during night were first sleek and fat, then gaunt and lean, Pharaoh thought, but is it any concern of mine? (Genesis, 41, 1–4). In his dream diary, William Burroughs relates, in addition to innocuous visions of doors opening, meals, meetings with relatives, a few puzzling fantasies: *'Jerry Evans is driving at reckless speed down a one-way street going the wrong way. We narrowly miss a truck. Usually in dreams of fast driving my father is at the wheel. Is Jerry my father? The danger seems very real. No feeling that this is just a dream.'*[2] Other visions frighten the sleeper because they look incomprehensible. What is this huge, dazzling image made of different metals? Why is it shattered to fragments by a stone? How is it possible for the stone to grew into a great mountain filling the whole earth?, Nabuchadnezzar wondered (Daniel, 2). Burroughs again: *'Dark inside the house. Heavy palpable darkness of danger. I go down to the living room. Here and there are plates of glass with wedges bitten out. Lucien eating glass on Bedford Street in the Village. I open the front door, outside is daylight but it is night inside.'*

If dreams have a meaning, or give warning of an impending danger, the dreamer may be in peril as long as these fantasies remain enigmatic, and it sounds perfectly reasonable to look for an accurate explanation. The collections of ready-made interpretations pass over too many disturbing points to be really satisfactory; referring to them is not sufficient to overcome one's apprehensions. Reporting to someone else helps to master immediate, instinctive fears. In Sumerian documents the same word was used to indicate a dream account addressed to another person, the interpretation offered by that person and the solution given to the vision's enigma, especially the removal of its damaging consequences. From a functional point of view, telling, receiving an external judgement and taking advantage of that opinion, were identical. This example illustrates the curative power of speech and the importance of an attentive listening. But relatives or friends do not give an interpretation, they merely play down dreams' most frightening aspects; their soothing words look more intuitive than authoritative. Real worries require much more, they ask for a trained person's intervention. In such instances, taking an exegete's advice is a call for help; it is hoped that the specialist will bring some relief from the power of the dream. What is expected is not only a capacity to listen, but, more important, an ability to give an 'objective' answer.

Professional interpreters could adopt as a slogan Prometheus' saying in Aeschylus' play: the hero glories in having taught people to discern what aspects of their life come to the forefront in their dreams. An expert's request is repeatedly mentioned in texts treating of dreams. Joseph encounters Pharaoh's servants, who are in a very low state: they tell him that they have had a dream – three wine branches ripening into grapes, three baskets of white bread – and that there was no one to interpret it. Joseph could have kept silent, but he chose to advise them and ease their anxiety. Pharaoh in turn is upset by the fat and lean cows: he summons various Egyptian magicians and sages, and then Joseph himself. Nebuchadnezzar, impressed by the huge image seen in dreams, can no longer sleep and begs for an interpretation. Tacitus tells how king Ptolemy Soter, troubled by the incomprehensible orders a colossus had given him during sleep, did not stop consulting exegetes until someone explained the meaning of the message.[3]

The texts we have just mentioned date from antiquity, but even in our own time many conceive of dreams as messages addressed to sleepers in the form of a riddle. Siberian tribes attribute to dreams a twofold role: they are meant to disclose the origins of afflictions, individual or collective misfortunes, accidents and other serious events. At the same time they provide an explanation and show what solution or what cure, in the case of illness, will prove effective. As soon as they have seen unexpected, perturbing images during the night, they look for a diagnosis.

Siberian tribes and other small groups that live like them are exceptions in our time. Are not we allowed to contrast the soothsayers, whose role was eminent in pre-industrial communities, and our doctors, psychoanalysts or other scientists, all specialists who have undergone extensive training? Today, as in the past, dream interpreters must analyse their clients' fantasies and help find a solution to a state of anxiety. But the differences are more important than such superficial correspondences. Psychoanalysts meet with resistances to be resolved by degrees, over a long period. Dreams help them to detect how, thanks to a series of strange but comprehensible operations, a deep meaning has been replaced by a fantasy. Even if they know what is at stake, their task is to help their patients to disclose their own truth, not to deliver a clear-cut diagnosis. On the other hand, past and present soothsayers are urged to talk about and explain the signs involved in a dream. Their precise, factual answers must alleviate a dramatic, sometimes unbearable uneasiness and provide their patients with some guidance.

The methods and aims of soothsayers and doctors are far apart. Let us leave the point aside for the moment, and return to it later. Ancient soothsayers, it is important to stress, were professionals, and good professionals at that. Is there an insuperable gap between their training and that of modern scientists? Though not medical doctors, Joseph and Daniel lacked neither competence nor skill. Daniel had received a good intellectual education, knew the king's court well, and was in touch with his colleagues, the official Babylonian diviners. The writings left by two interpreters, Flavius Josephus and Artemidorius, clarify the skills required in their profession. In the two study manuals he wrote for the instruction of future dream interpreters, Artemidorius described his own training. He spent many years with practising exegetes, listening carefully, even when he disagreed, because 'there was no other way of becoming skilled', but he also read all the treatises on the topic. He agreed with Flavius Josephus on the necessity for a good soothsayer to be learned.[4] A perfect knowledge of one's own culture's fundamental texts and traditions was crucial, but not entire, for it was also indispensable, when receiving foreigners, to learn about their customs, uses and language because these are the basis of dream images and word associations. All symbols and figures, Artemidorius insisted, must be considered from the viewpoint of local costumes and circumstances, the interpreter's task consisting of establishing connections ('a bridge' was his word) between the vision's content, the dreamer's life and the social context. No psychoanalyst would disapprove of such a statement: Freud's followers link allegories and symbols to their patient's specific environment,[5] and might endorse Artemidorius' slogan: 'Adapt your interpretation to the dreamer's personality.'

Using one's practical good sense has long been a rule of dream reading. Reports made by the dreamers must be related to their place of origin, residence, age and social condition. The dreamer's status is also of relevance. As already noted in the *Iliad* (II, 83), there is a great difference between kings' and ordinary citizens' dreams. Both may have the same vision. But if the latter dream of public affairs, it is only a dissimulation of some personal worry, and their delusion must be read as such. On the other hand, a royal vision can encode actual concerns about the state, its government, its security or its welfare. Identical images lend themselves to various interpretations according to the sleepers' rank and condition. Artemidorius' warnings are not outmoded: contemporary books relate the reading of political dreams to the sleeper's effective responsibilities.

Daniel was good at conveying an exegesis without frightening his public. When Nebuchadnezzar solicited his opinion of a dream he remained silent for a moment, then asked permission to give his point of view, keeping the king in suspense in the most respectful manner. His interpretation was bad news for Nebuchadnezzar, but his formula seemed to imply greater evil for the king's enemies than for Nebuchadnezzar himself (4, 19). Psychoanalysts, Freud insisted,[6] have to communicate as tactfully as possible with their patients. According to their reactions they will have recourse to persuasion or authority, but they will not go directly to the core of the pathology. Tact is a rule in the matter. Let us summarize Daniel's diagnosis: Take your dream as a good omen. Your foes will be wiped out. But before that, you will undergo terrible hardships. In this way you will become strong enough to crush your adversaries. Psychoanalysts warn their clients: You will get rid of your obsession or impotence. Yet it is first necessary to understand what your dreams express. This may be extremely painful. Don't worry, you will then be cured. Psychoanalysts learn how to be always alert and attentive to seemingly insignificant detail. However important, technical skill matters less than psychological intuition, concern, patience and 'a free human outlook' – to borrow Freud's words.

Experience, cautiousness, attention to cultural traditions are not sufficient to risk a comparison between soothsayers and psychoanalysts, for it is also imperative to examine their particular procedures. Artemidorius urged future soothsayers to question their clients carefully to be sure they had been given the whole dream. Nothing, however minor, should be omitted; small particulars could prove to be the most significant part of the dreams. Some psychoanalysts remain silent in order to allow their patients to make a free association of ideas and impressions, but many consider it their duty to pick out hesitations or lapses and ask for more details. Dreaming of a sailor during the night seems innocuous enough, but the vision's meaning changes when the therapist elicits the name of, for children, a frightening figure: Captain Hook.[7]

When a report was obviously fragmentary, Artemidorius advised his disciples to connect it to related information or to the accounts of other dreams. Siberian shamans and Native American medicine men had recourse to the same technique: they estimated what parts of the visions could be accepted, and what particulars should be added to make a diagnosis. Psychoanalysts are theoretically opposed to such practice. In their view it is the patients' business to struggle with themselves until they find a solution to their problems. However, in a few instances, when a patient remains silent and cannot correlate his or her fantasies with anything else, they do not hesitate to ply the patient with questions. To quote D. W. Winnicott's colourful expression, they 'fish around for dreams'.[8] In some instances Freud himself imposed his personal reading. A man in his thirties remembered dreaming when he was only four of two big white pears: he was given one fruit while the other was left on the windowsill. There was much more in the patient's report, notably a combination with a motherly dream. Freud did not notice the latter. Mother's breast was his verdict: it had been sucked (one pear to the child) but there was still a desire to suck more (another pear left).

Freud's interference in the case of the dream of two pears, and his partial reading, illustrate an important aspect of analytical practice: interpretations are seldom conclusive and there is often room for other reflections. Artemidorus, a very cautious, flexible practitioner, would have agreed. He recommended to 'employ in each case some logical and convincing explanation', while advising against being too confident in logical connections. He found it crucial to ponder all the minute aspects of a dream, but insisted that a general view of its meaning was indispensable. He mentioned several archetypes of general symbols, but was quick to add that no sign had an ubiquitous, permanent meaning. Some of his examples of dream ambiguity are amusing. (During the night seven pregnant women dreamed they gave birth to a dragon; the theme, borrowed from folklore, was common, but each individual woman had her own unique past and present, and deserved a personal interpretation.)

Artemidorius was particularly original in his use of vocabulary. Most words, he realized, have various meanings, and by similarity evoke other words. 'Etymology should always be used' as well as puns and resemblances; it is wise to consider the whole sequence linking a given term to its possible causes and effects and to explore proverbs, myths, plays on words and number combinations deriving from an expression. A key feature of psychoanalytical theory is what Freud named the 'dream-work'. During sleep, he contended, dreams transform thoughts or wishes into the story the sleeper will remember when he awakes. The process consists in reducing an abstract entity to a tangible emblem or to one of its parts, replacing an entity by something from another domain and transforming something into what it is not. A patient, for instance, dreamed of standing on a seaside pier, but the analyst's insistence made him translate *pier* into *peer, sea* into *see* and acknowledge a voyeurist fancy.[9] Without offering a system as elaborated as Freud's, Artemidorius anticipated this strategy. He explained how a person, a child, for instance, could represent an entire group. Pondering the word *winning* he showed how a euphoric impression could be substituted for an individual name pronounced identically but provoking a depressing sensation. He also mentioned instances of contradiction, the term *curing* being used to camouflage *dying.*

Artemidorius deserves close study because his *Interpretation of Dreams*, plagiarized down to the eighteenth century, was the soothsayers' bible. He and his followers were not spiritists bluntly overwhelmed by nebulous intuitions, but careful observers of their contemporaries' concerns. Flavius Josephus' self-portrait throws light on their state of mind. During the dreadful period of the war with the Romans, Flavius was simultaneously having dreams, fighting, interpreting his or his friends' visions, informing his comrades in arms of divine messages and praying. Self-control, calm, concentration, were not the only qualities of traditional exegetes: these men were real experts. They had gone through long, serious training, were keen to calm their clients' distresses, and their dream analyses were far from valueless.

It is not a question of method but rather of form of thought. Deities or supernatural forces were always in the background of ancient methods. Rationalist theorists like Aristotle or Artemidorius conceived of dreams as messages sleepers sent to themselves to emphasize impending dangers or to indicate health problems. Yet all believed in the possible interference of an external agent – God, a genie or any other vague entity. Artemidorius, who found in dreams information about his clients' present state, relied also on the predictive power of visions. Beside sensible exegesis he was able to write: 'Someone dreamed he had an iron penis. He fathered a son who killed him. For iron is consumed by the rust it produces.'

In modern thought there is little, if any, place for unearthly beings. Even though at night sleepers exclusively fantasize about their personal worries or hopes, they accept the predominant model of analysis based on functions, conflicts and relations. Psychoanalysis is arguably a science, but it was born in a scientific context and its procedures, close to the medical or psychological ones, define its positiveness. Some, today, will undergo a long, uncertain analytical treatment while yet looking into a textbooks and hoping for a quick answer, but they know these to be mutually exclusive strategies.

Moneymakers?

Buying a dream manual is less expensive than resorting to a psychoanalyst. Still, money is involved in both cases. Those who seek for the resolution of disturbances triggered by dreams must pay. Freud did not avoid the topic, but he tackled it in an abrupt manner: 'I regret to say it, but analytic therapy is almost inaccessible to poor people. Little can be done to remedy this.'[10] Remuneration, he added, is imperative because therapists need it to live and because sufferers do not take seriously what is free. Such motives sound reasonable and banal; they apply to all goods and services and miss two important questions: the risk of exploitation, and the therapists' benefits other than mere defrayal.

Many cope with their dreams, Artemidorius observed, but those frightened by a strange or menacing delusion are in need of help. It would be easy to write an history of abuse through dream interpretation. Here is a typical case. In Naples, until the end of the eighteenth century, priests who ran lotteries for church funds published *La Smorfia,* a pamphlet combining dream images with corresponding lottery numbers: 'If you see yourself walking or flying or whatsoever, play number x.' Among credulous people prone to believe in miracles and instant riches, the trick worked perfectly well.

This verged on dishonesty. Others were far from scrupulous too, earning their living thanks to dream interpretation. In Mesopotamia, ancient Egypt and Greece, the Roman empire, during the Middle Ages and even in modern times, at least in North Africa and the Middle East, there were temples or shrines where people could have heavenly inspired dreams. Sometimes a god or a saint visited them during sleep and cured their illness or allayed their fears. Sometimes the same gave advice about a serious decision or about one's future. Occasionally the visitors simply sought a divine revelation. The practice is well documented, thanks to the steles erected by satisfied devotees at Aesculapian shrines[11] and the biographies of healing saints. What comes to the fore is the length of the enterprise. The expected figure did not appear at once: his devotees had to stay for several days in the temple, where they paid for their maintenance. Some spent a long time there. The *Miracles of Artemios* mention a carpenter who, while staying at Artemios' church, 'executed with care many joinery works', presumably in return for hospitality and subsistence. Medical care was provided for the disabled, again for a fee. The cure could be direct and immediate, the supernatural instruction perfectly clear. But the healer could also recommend a treatment or deliver vague directions. Thereafter the visitor was obliged to turn to an intepreter for help, and, if she or he was ill, to follow the medical procedure.

Patients who have spent tedious years undergoing psychoanalysis often complain about its duration and price. Inscriptions at Aesculapian temples reveal the case of sufferers who not only had stayed there for a long time but had returned to the shrine. There seems to have been, in the Western and Mediterranean world, a long-ingrained habit of spending money on dream exegesis. Reporting one's visions may be initially painful, but it can turn out to be relieving. When not forgotten, a dreadful dream is a burden the sleeper would like to be rid of. Once told, the dream becomes less powerful. Some find it necessary to apologize: 'It sounds a bit silly; I was impressed for no valid reason' – yet they have been happy to report their fantasies. Other dreams manifest hidden desires, and an account gives them a corporeity, represents them through figures and sensations. A report prolongs the fantasy while allowing the dreamer to modify and even embellish it. Paraphrasing Freud, we can say that an account helps to discharge a pre-existing tension, and such a procedure has a price. There is more. Dreamtelling is an incentive to evoke other fantasies. The relationship between a patient who confesses what she or he has fancied during sleep and the analyst grows to be more and more subjective, at least on the client's side. Such awakening of emotions leads to transference – a displacement on to the therapist of inclinations or apprehensions dating from the past.

Freud recommended analysts to remain perfectly objective. This may be the reason why he reduced the therapist's profit to money and did not consider other advantages. A few remarks disclose his awareness of something else, 'the patient's influence on the analyst's unconscious feelings'.[12] Artemidorius learned much about his profession by listening: his books are filled with visions by his clients. Psychoanalysts are more involved in their work than soothsayers because analysis usually goes on for several years. Weekly meetings result in nothing but complicity: therapist and patient form a pair unified by the dream account; their association brings about interpretations that anyone else might find difficulty in understanding.

Even though pretending to remain objective, analysts are affected by their clients' fantasies, and, like Artemidorius, they improve their expertise in the course of a cure. Since the medical profession initially had a poor opinion of them, psychoanalysts formed their own professional societies. They still belong to study groups, organize seminars and publish in journals. Their patients' dreams provide them with the raw materiel that is to be dissected and discussed. The symbolic benefits of the profession – delivering a paper, publishing a book – are neither negligible nor open to damning criticism. Both Freud and Jung first made their name as dream interpreters.

Gullibility Exploiters?

Our nocturnal visions, Jonathan Swift contended in his poem 'On Dreams' (1728), 'all are mere productions of the brain, / and fools consult inter- preters in vain'. This was a short, pungent restatement of a warning endlessly repeated, almost with the same words for many centuries. Since antiquity commentators have never stopped warning their contemporaries against dream interpreters. Cicero was among the fiercest opponents of diviners and foretellers. Dreams, he contended, are usually very simple, everyone can understand them, no mediator is needed. Making fun of contradictory exegeses based on the same visions and offering different but equally erroneous interpretations, he gave amusing examples of misleading interpretations. Two Olympic competitors had a dream. The first dreamed of driving a four-horse chariot, the second of being an eagle. These were declared favourable omens, but it turned out they were not. The specialists were obliged to explain why: in the former case it was because the man, during sleep, had run before the race; in the latter, because eagles pursue other birds, and thus come after. Dreams, Cicero concluded, 'would of themselves have no influence and would rather be despised if certain philosophers had not taken them under their special patronage', and, in order to be reputed above the common sort, made people believe they enjoyed a very special gift.

When he mocked the soothsayers, thanks to an absurd verdict, Cicero mingled (willingly?) future predictions made via dreams and the *interpretation* of dreams. This has been a long-lasting confusion (one still echoed in modern times). In Shakespeare's *Cymbeline*, for example, soldiers ask a soothsayer for his prediction for the forthcoming battle. Having dreamed of an eagle, the man, delivering his verdict in a roundabout way, foresaw a victory. Despite such a favourable prophecy, the battle was lost. But Cicero, having been educated in a philosophical tradition highly sceptical about the divinatory power of dreams, should have distinguished two distinct undertakings – vaticination and dream exegesis. Soothsayers, the Roman highbrows insisted, gave complicated advice only to make their clients forget that dreams are available to everybody and in order to charge a high price for their predictions. Those who mentioned examples likely to prove the veracity of dream foretelling did not take the time to consider that they pointed out mere coincidence and did not prove anything. However, though they did not praise dream prophecy, Greek and Roman intellectuals took dreams seriously, as can been inferred from the many texts they wrote on the topic.

A few manifested a secular conception. Synesius of Cyrene conceived of dreams as internal dialogues with himself. When he had to reach an important decision he took a close look at the question before going to bed. The next day he knew what to do. Many believed in divine messages delivered in religious sanctuaries, but did not trust the so-called 'inspired' exegetes. Plato was typical of such a position; his was an enlightened, cognitive point of view, which he expressed in *Timaeus, 72*:

> It is the task of a man when his intellectual powers are at their peak to ponder, once he has gathered them in his mind, the words spoken by the divine power in dream or waking vision as well as the visions this power has disclosed; then to analyze them by the

use of reason in order to discern what they may signify and for whom in the future, the past or the present and if they give warning of evil or good. As for the man who has been and is still in a state of frenzy it is not his task to interpret what he has seen.

There were, everybody conceded, a few troublesome dreams. But who were the best interpreters if not the dreamers themselves, provided they were able to brush aside physical impressions and discern what scattered, confused images and sounds stand for? Avicenna, Aristotle's distant follower, devised an ingenious system likely to help most individuals to understand their dreams: look first at the images identical to objects, landscapes, panoramas or situations you have previously experienced. These tell you very simple things about your daily concerns. As for the enigmatic visions, you have to evaluate them. How? When the dreams seem obscure, clues for their interpretation are most probably latent in them. A person of well-developed cognitive power must make up her or his mind and find the meaning of a dream within the dream itself.

Let us remember Plato's mistrust of dreams. He believed they provided the vulgar with an opportunity to indulge in libidinous images. Only the refined were able to consider their dreams carefully and to profit from them. Literate Greeks and Romans made fun of soothsayers, and all those gullible enough to ascribe to dreams a special significance, a means to forecast the future. Scrutinized by expert minds, they alleged, dreams are clear and useful, but those of ordinary rank prefer fantastic, deceitful promises. Contrasting pairs like credulity/clear-mindedness express indirectly a class conflict: the lower class, the upper-class think, swallow everything. Such distinction was still made by eighteenth- and nineteenth-century scientists engaged in systematic research about dreams. Freud endorsed it when he stressed the cost – but did not allude to the time consumption – involved in psychoanalysis.

The rational approach of ancient philosophers and modern doctors simplified the dream enigma. The recommended procedure consisted in dismissing incongruous, obscure images and keeping only that which could be interpreted. Here came the analytical revolution: what looks confused, contradictory, inconsistent is, Freud argued, as significant as what is clear. Not everybody was convinced, even those who had recourse to dreamtelling in the course of effecting psychological cures. There are analysts who detect in wild, nonsensical fantasies nothing more than a reflection of their patient's chaotic state of mind. What is the nature of dreams: the question is still open. Do we merely speak to ourselves during sleep, as Synesius thought? Is there something in us, an unconscious force that tries to surface? Let us stop here, this would bring us back to the conflicting dream theories developed from antiquity through to our time. Dreams, as I have suggested, are fascinating inasmuch as they do not lend themselves to all-encompassing systems.

Joseph and Daniel scorned the official diviners who were unable to give their sovereign a satisfying answer. Psychoanalysts affiliated to various schools distrust one other. But what determines who is called a serious professional and who a charlatan? The dominant mode of interpreting the world, the cultural attitudes, prejudices and curiosities of a given period, play a crucial role, Freud met with quick success because his ideas were acceptable at the outset of the twentieth century. This is only a precondition, not an explanation. Different, often conflicting, forms of therapy based on the analysis of dreams prove to be effective and have good results, although there is no clear understanding of how they succeed. This is possibly because those upset or frightened by the strange, unaccountable unfolding of their dreams find in a treatment, whatever its presuppositions, a way of coping with their anxiety. Good professionals are those who introduce their patients to an acceptable, reassuring interpretation. As for those who feel no noctur-nal apprehension, they will be their own dream exegetes.

Conclusion

After almost two centuries of close observation and clinical control, dreams have not been mastered. They intrigue us, but we are as unable as the ancients to explain their functioning. Do we really need to understand them? Our relationship with our dreams is as emotional as it is intellectual. We all know from vivid personal experience the long-lasting impression, often upsetting or pleasant, they are likely to have on us. Some people are even dramatically affected by them. 'My dreams became the substance of my life', Coleridge once wrote. He spoke of his '*Dræmatis Personae*', uncanny nocturnal figures able to perform unexpected scenes in 'somnial and morphean space'. His was not an exceptional case. Speaking on television,[1] a 50-year-old woman, Willa Woolston, confessed: 'All my life the first sensation as I wake has been fear.' Such obsession provoked by images that crossed one's mind during sleep verges on pathology, Coleridge had difficulty recovering his 'true self', and for many years the memory of a miserable childhood haunted Willa Woolston's nights.

Since his patients' stability was often threatened by nightmares, Freud took such agonies seriously. But what could be done with sufferers who

had no memory of the figures perceived during sleep and were left with excruciating impressions deprived of images or sound? 'I just felt', noted Willa Woolston, 'apprehension, dread' and nothing else. If we have dreams every night, we do not always remember them. It is a paradox of that mysterious mental activity; dreams exist for us inasmuch as they are reported. Ill-defined sensations of discomfort or of happiness, not unusual on waking, are felt in various ways to be related to a mere physical reaction or to a dream.

Let us consider two examples. After dreaming of a fight with a living skeleton, Robert Southey was not only scared, his body was affected; his dream had left him with a diffused pain, as if he had been bruised. Conversely, a 30-year-old executive awoke in great form:

> *'I dreamed I was lying on my back. Leandra Neri entered, coming from the right, as on a theatre stage. She is my colleague's sister, I saw*

her twice only, briefly and casually, always dressed in black. In my vision she was wearing a turquoise blouse and casual trousers. She lay across my legs and talked about herself. I did not catch the words, but it was peaceful and soothing. Just remembering the dream made me happy for two days.'

It will be argued that affective or somatic factors account for the after-effects we have just mentioned. Southey's mattress was probably hard and lumpy, and we should not wonder that a young man was in a sentimental mood. Such motivations may explain a sense of hopeless discomfort or of surprising well-being. But emotive or corporeal reactions justify neither the images or sounds perceived by the sleepers, nor the disconcerting stories they contrive. To feel aches all over at night does not necessarily lead to fantasies about skeletons, and there is no reason to enliven one's night with the visit of the almost unknown sister of a colleague.

Unexpected, oddly combined figures in dreams are also elusive. William Blake emphasized their fugitive nature in *America, a Prophecy:* 'In vain the dreamer grasps the joyful images, they fly seen in obscured traces . . .'. One of his etchings, *The Dream of Thiralatha* (opposite), depicts such transience. Thiralatha, the symbol in Blake's mythology of liberated love, is relaxing in the position of a sitting sleeper, head bent on her knees. A semi-oval shape, a cavern's inner wall or a huge wave, encircles her. Just above her head and behind her, two silhouettes are sketched. These faint, shadowy profiles represent ephemeral visions crossing the woman's mind. Dreamed caverns and waves are often associated by psychoanalysts to the uterus and the amniotic liquid. The sleeping Thiralatha might experience an imaginary return to her mother's womb. The soothing, agreeable character of her vision is emphasized by a little bird flying to the right. But hers is not only a pleasant feeling, it is accompanied by another image: she fancies a slim naked woman holding and kissing a child. Herself in her mother's arms? Or more likely herself with her baby?

Blake's etching renders perfectly the effect produced by a pleasant dream. There is first an emotion, an intense but imprecise feeling of being profoundly concerned. Blake's character is relaxing; vague figures flit through her mind. Their origin may be purely physiological. But neurological phenomena, rooted in the depths of our mental life, are intrinsically resistant to the efforts of language to apprehend them. We would be unable to tell what we dreamed at night if there were neither images nor narrative elements. What remains in our mind is visual, aural, and can be reported. At the same time it is evanescent. If Blake's young woman has perceived agreeable, delicate figures, their identity is ambiguous. Any attempt to explain what she has seen will be partial and not fully satisfactory.

Although they elude our attempts to describe them adequately, dreams matter because they arrange unpredictable meetings, bring to the fore forgotten, at times dead, people and put us into awkward situations. We feel involved, we take part in what is happening, though we are unable to control the progress of our vision. Such fleetingness has long been a lasting worry: it is mentioned in the most ancient documents. Countless specialists have attempted to show how dreams form. Unfortunately there is no way of dealing scientifically with impressions that can be neither recorded directly nor repeated. Our observations, limited to the effects produced on our behaviour while we are asleep and after we awake, are peripheral, do not 'prove' anything, and can be used to buttress conflicting systems.

Here we are faced with the most puzzling aspect of dreams. They exist independently of any particular period: something fundamentally similar connects them throughout the centuries. Yet attitudes to dreams evolve in different times and places. The Babylonians, Egyptians, Greeks and Romans dreamed like us. At night their minds jumped from one topic to another, they walked with a person who, suddenly, was the same but also another, they entered a building that turned out to be nothing but a hole. However, the scenery of their delusions, the people they met, the perils they had to confront, were different from ours: deities sometimes visited them, they were asked to dinner by kings or mythical heroes, they had to fight monsters.

In his early work Freud gave greater place to personal affects in dream-formation. But after the First World War he became more and more aware of the importance of cultural factors. Explaining how sleepers tackle some of their hidden difficulties with material borrowed from their surroundings, he confirmed what contemporary sociologists were contending: the landscapes and characters we see during sleep are subject to passing influences and contingent fashions, like any representation. When reporting our dreams we place them in an environment similar to ones we know. In ancient Greece travel-dreams were associated with horses and carts, in seventeenth-century England with ships, in the nineteenth century with trains, and today with aeroplanes.

The images available for dreams are produced by a society, but there is more to it than that. It is also the society that creates the intellectual tools needed to give dreams a meaning. This widens the gap between different periods. Dream interpretations evolve throughout millennia; previous explanations become irrelevant and conjure up, at best, an impression of naïvety. Ancient people wondered whether such delusions were signs sent by external powers, as the majority believed, or were physical reactions caused by internal processes, as was defended by a minority. In the intellectual atmosphere of antiquity such debate was not absurd. Constraining the former to identify the senders of nocturnal messages and to classify the various types of divine instructions, these helped to clarify the relationship between gods and human beings. And it obliged the advocates of bodily origin to examine the dreams and dreamers carefully and to write accurate proceedings.

The personal, idiosyncratic formation of dreams is widely accepted today. They are considered psychic phenomena alien to any objective assessment but amenable to scientific investigation. Psychological research has shaped our conception of dreams, especially since psychoanalysis has used them to explain how our unconscious works. In my view they are a normal part of sleep and an imaginative mental activity: it is our manner of thinking while asleep. If our perception of nocturnal life is slightly more precise than it was a few centuries ago, our ideas about dreams are neither better nor more justified. What has changed is merely our way of dealing with sleep, of describing and understanding it. Infatuated with scientific terms and arguments, we are tempted to think that our ancestors relied on unchecked data and superstitious beliefs. However, modern theories are far from being firmly established. Some of our contemporaries claim that dreams are the guardians of sleep and camouflage improper wishes likely to disturb our night. Others, on the contrary, claim that they deal with forbidden wishes censored during the day but free to make their presence felt when the process of repression is gone. I am not disturbed by this discrepancy because the various systems have recourse to psychological terms that are part of our vocabulary, but such phrasing would have been hardly comprehensible when thought was organized on moral, divinatory or theological principles.

The description of dreams, of their codes, of their themes and symbolic structures, is framed by the concepts accessible to the majority in a given period. Theorizing nocturnal activities is nothing but using the available stock of ideas and notions to characterize vagaries that cannot be adequately represented. The same is true of many aspects of our life, for instance, the reasons why the world exists or why it is as it is. These metaphysical questions cannot be solved by direct, quantifiable examination. And such are the problems related to the origin, nature and meaning of dreams. Take a simple puzzle: is there really a human free will if, during sleep, another, hidden part of ourselves, or our organs, or some external power, monitors our thoughts? Any answer will be based on unproveable statements.

In their study of dreams, analysts and scientists must consider to what extent dreamers take part in the creation of their fantasies and consider whether sleeping 'thought' is deliberate or accidental. But in the absence of evidence, all they can do is to make assumptions grounded on their epoch's philosophical principles. Consider the executive's vision given above. Imagine it was reported *c.* 1850, when many people regarded dreams as useless perceptions stored in the brain and 'unloaded' during sleep. At the time specialists would have said that our young man looked at his colleague's sister absentmindedly, and, not interested in her, removed her image at night. What was worth noticing were the odds and ends pointlessly registered by his eye and the cleansing done by the brain. With his *Interpretation of Dreams* Freud introduced the idea of 'displacement', or the substitution of one image by another. The notion is now widely diffused, even among those who do not support Freud's hypotheses in their original form. The colleague's sister, analysts would contend, symbolizes another person, who can be identified by examining seemingly unimportant details, such as the theatre or casual clothes.

Theories about the origin and signification of dreams provide us with an analytical vocabulary. We speak of the unconscious, of dreamwork and wish-fulfilment, whereas in the nineteenth century the subject was spoken of in terms of the association of ideas and images developing logically one from the other. The terms an epoch uses are culturally conditioned and affect its understanding of past and present dreams. Nineteenth-century specialists, brushing aside imagination, looked for objects or living beings seen in waking life that were assembled at night according to formal similarities. We search for secret desires and unconscious needs distorted and hidden among uncoordinated series of events.

Some do not hesitate to apply modern concepts to ancient dreams. Is it not, arguably, an incorrect method? After dreaming during sleep of Ulysses' return, Penelope thought she had been sent a favourable omen by a deity. She would have regarded as meaningless any reference to an hallucinatory satisfaction of her desires. Are we allowed to read back our own conceptions into ancient periods? In principle, no. Habits, ideas and images were very different then. But the notions we use are our only access to past visions. If we admit that Penelope believed in a communication with Mt Olympus, we cannot claim she received a heavenly message. However anachronistic with respect to Greek convictions, we are obliged to put forward a psychological interpretation of this dream.

Owing to their quirky, disruptive nature, dreams are enigmas. Alone they do not speak. Many are content with summing up the strange ingredients they have put together. A few look for an explanation, but any exegesis is necessarily phrased in current language. Let us go back to Southey's aggressive skeleton. For those who conceive of dreams as warnings given either by an external power or by our own body, what matters is the core of the message. Getting rid of secondary elements and focusing on the innermost part of the vision, these people will think: 'I have seen a representation of death.' On the other hand, those who give greater place to psychology will search for minute, seemingly irrelevant, particulars likely to shed light on their inner self. Subjectivity, philosophical or religious creeds and available concepts interfere in the construction of dream accounts. Telling or writing about one's dreams results in regulating them according to pre-established patterns.

Reporting a dream is not sufficient to calm an anxious sleeper. If, according to the traditional view, the skeleton is a presage, does it mean that Southey is about to die? Or that a secret disease is gradually eating away his body? Or that he will overcome an impending danger? And if, as psychoanalysis suggests, it is a product of his unconscious, what shameful yearning does it conceal? People have always been anxious to disclose the secrets of their visions. After all, the numerous dreambooks that figure prominently among the oldest written documents have been copied out over and again throughout the centuries.

Concise, often sententious, such manuals offer clear-cut solutions to oversimplified dream accounts. Since consulting them is seldom satisfying, worried sleepers much prefer turning to dream exegetes. Diviners in the Bible appear as respected men. The authority of psychoanalysts is well established in our own time, but, as a rule, soothsayers, taxed with the charge of exploiting the gullible, have earned themselves a wretched reputation. Yet many go to them for advice, and their answers, however ambiguous, often put their clients' minds at ease. By questioning their clients, and making them clarify their impressions, dream experts do play a part in establishing how dreams must be told.

In a sphere as imprecise as the realm of dreams, no clear distinction can be made between evidence and interpretation. Far from being transparent documents, the accounts given by sleepers are constructed and mediated creations. Dream reports are first biased by the individuals' choice to acknowledge them or not, to describe them as accurately as possible or to conceal embarrassing features. The frankest cannot but communicate their visions in accordance with the patterns defined by dream specialists, or by the narrative models accessible to their contemporaries. And the accepted knowledge about the nature of sleep and dreams determines how the latter should be interpreted.

Dream records are to a large extent predictable tales or socially organized fiction: it is easy to arrange them in relation to well-established types. The dreamers' waking activities, their desires, concerns and expectations, the people and places they know, supply the background. Against such settings, dreams deal with subjects as banal and universal as food, travel, love, sex, disease, death. *'I am sitting at a table with a friend I have never seen before but who is familiar'* or *'I walk into an empty room where I am welcome by a handsome man, I try to meet his eyes but he is no longer there'* are fugacious delusions many have experienced. Most dreamed matters are commonplaces already familiar to thousands. Our attempts at expressing them comes with, and from, the set of theoretical principles current in our own times.

Does this mean that we have no access to our irreducibly opaque nocturnal life? Or that the flashes crossing our sleeping mind are systematically reordered, in daytime, after the manner of the narrative mode?

Although all we can tell about our sleeping life is a product of how our epoch thinks and instructs us to report on it, our dreams are neither a mere object contrived by the circle we live in nor a mere fiction concocted after we awake. There is a gap between what we perceive in sleep and what we are able to communicate. Our report is only an aspect of the impression we experienced, but the little we tell makes a difference. If we were unable to say anything we would know neither that we dream nor that our dreams matter to us. 'Intelligent' machines have reached an extraordinary level of development: some are able not only to answer abstruse queries but to adapt to the specific needs of those facing them. However, robots will never dream because they are built according to a pre-established pattern. Selfish, idiosyncratic, our dreams are private psychological and corporal manifestations. As such they elude any form of modelling. They are ours, but we have no way of explaining the form they finally take. If we grasp in them traces of our day's activities and pick out associations or thought-chains, we are baffled by their uncontrollable succession of accidents, turnabouts and abrupt switches in scene and character. During sleep even those people most deprived of imagination become creative, at time poetical and can even gain a sense of humour they normally lack. The less inspired visit countries they will never see, travel through space, perform acts they condemn or secretly would like to carry out. They behave as if they were another person. 'When I dream, I am Ulysses', a young lady confesses. Analysts will diagnose the desire to be a man or the search for adventure. They may be right, but they will miss the delight there can be in transgressing boundaries and changing identities – being another person for a while, a privilege life never grants us.

Reporting dreams helps us to master our emotions, take stock of ourselves, prolong an agreeable impression, marvel at the wonderful plot we have improvised – all expressed in words. Dreamtelling channels a flux, an evolving process into a text unlikely to exhaust the vision's potential. However, while betraying them, accounts allow us to give dreams a place in our waking life. Some deplore such a compromise. It is a contraction, but it is also our sole possibility to appreciate the inventive capacity, the play of allusions, metaphors, displacements and puns at work in our sleeping minds. Not all remember their visions or bother to describe them. Those who do it manifest the variety of human symbolic intelligence there is. Telling a dream is as enjoyable as listening to a dream account – and neither the storyteller nor the listener wonders whether the report is wholly faithful to the original.

References

Introduction

1 S. T. Coleridge, *Collected Letters*, 6 vols, ed. E. L. Griggs (Oxford, 1966), 14 August 1803.

2 'On Dreams', in *Essays and Hymns*, 2 vols (London, 1930), § 12.

3 *On Soul*, XLVIII, 3.

4 Macrobius was the author of a *Commentary on the Dream of Scipio*, at the same time a gloss over Cicero's treatise on dreams, *Scipio's Dream*, and a series of personal notes on sleep.

5 Collections of dreams can be found in Ignaz Jezower, *Das Buch der Traüme* (Berlin, 1925), Calvin S. Hall, *The Meaning of Dreams* (New York, 1966), Stephen Brook, *The Oxford Book of Dreams* (Oxford, 1987), Harry T. Hunt, *Multiplicity of Dreams: Memory, Imagination and Consciousness* (New Haven, CT, 1989).

One: Dreams and Imagination

1 See Frederick S. Perls, *Gestalt Therapy* (Lafayette, 1969), David B. Cohen, *Sleep and Dreaming: Nature and Function* (Oxford and New York,

1979), and J.Allan Hobson, *The Dreaming Brain* (London, 1988).

2 *Choses vues* (14 November 1842).

3 'The Land of the Wandering Souls', *Arte* (14 April 2000).

4 Ignaz Jezower, *Das Buch der Traüme* (Berlin, 1925), p. 255.

5 Most data on shamanism are borrowed from Roberte Hamayon's
La chasse à l'âme. Esquisse d'une théorie du chamanisme sibérien (Paris,
1990).

6 Pio Franchi de' Cavalieri, *Note agiografiche* (Rome, 1909), III, pp. 102–3.

7 *Patrologiae Cursus Completus* (Paris, 1866), CX, c.841.

8 *Die unsichtbare Loge*, in *Werke* (Munich, 1976), I, pp. 224–5.

9 On the feeling of fractured identity in Romantic dream accounts see
Jennifer Ford, *Coleridge on Dreaming* (Cambridge, 1999).

10 *Flegeljahre*, in *Werke*, II, pp. 231–2.

11 *Il mestiere di vivere* (Turin, 1952), 22 January 1940.

12 Surrealism, a literary and artistic avant-garde movement, was launched
in 1924 with a *Manifesto* written by the group's leader, André Breton.

13 'Enquête sur le rêve', *Le Disque vert*, III/4 [Paris] (1925).

14 *Nuits sans nuit* (Paris, 1966).

Two: Who can tell us what Dreams are?

1 See Deirdre Barrett, ed., *Trauma and Dreams* (Cambridge, MA, 1997).

2 'On Sleep and Waking', 'On Dreams', 'On Divination through Dream'.

3 'On Sleep and Waking', 2, c.

4 *Confessions*, X, 30.

5 XVIII, 18.

6 476, c; 520, d; from 571, c to 572, a.

7 *Histories*, VI, 107.

8 *Hecuba*, 70; *Iphigeneia Among the Taurians*, 571–2.

9 *On Progress in Virtue*, XXXV; *On Philosophers' Opinion*, V, 1–2; *Socrates'*

Daemon, 13–14.

10 'On Dreams', in *Works* (London, 1931), V, p. 183 (I have modernized
Browne's spelling).

11 *A World of My Own: A Dream Diary* (London, 1992), pp. 3–7.

12 *The Interpretation of Dreams*, IV, p. 308 (in *The Standard Edition of the
Complete Psychological Works of Sigmund Freud*, ed. James Strachey,
London, 1953, cited below as *S.E.*).

13 *S.E.*, V, p. 686.

14 See Frederick C. Crews, *The Memory Wars: Freud's Legacy in Dispute*
(New York, 1997), an attack on Freud that provoked violent reactions.

15 *New Introductory Lectures on Psychoanalysis* (1933), *S.E.*, XXII, p. 73. Since
the word 'unconscious' is ambivalent and seems to imply that it is
the reverse of the conscious, Freud substituted it with the latin *id* = it;
the text quoted here concerns the *id*.

16 *On his Life*, I, 18.

17 *History of the Jewish War Against the Romans*, VII, 349.

18 *Principles of Psychology* (London, 1890), II, p. 294.

19 Jackson Steward Lincoln, *The Dream in Primitive Cultures* (London,
1935).

20 Carl Alfred Meier, 'The Dream in Ancient Greece', in G. E. von
Grunebaum and Roger Caillois, eds, *The Dream and Human Societies*
(Berkeley and Los Angeles, CA, 1966), p. 304.

21 I, 34; I, 107–8; III, 30; III, 124–5. It has been noted that all these bad
omens concern barbarians, that is to say, not Greeks.

22 III, 149.

23 VII, 14–18.

24 Leo Oppenheim, *The Interpretation of Dreams in the Ancient Near East*
(Philadelphia, 1956), p. 260.

25 'On Dreams', § 12.

26 'On Dreams', § 3.

27 Virgil S. Crisafulli and John W. Nesbitt, *The Miracles of St Artemios*

(Leiden and New York, 1997).

28 *Summa theologiae*, II, a, § 174.

29 *Summa theologiae*, II, a, § 95.

30 Jung's views on dreams are summarized (in English translation) in *The Structure and Dynamics of the Psyche* (in *The Collected Works of C. G. Jung*, VIII, ed. R.F.C. Hull, Princeton, NJ, 1960), and in *Man and His Symbols* (London, 1964).

31 Georges Perec, *La boutique obscure* (Paris, 1973), p. 64.

32 Dreambooks are widely read in Mediterranean countries, in Africa and in South America, where even the educated buy them – but which, of course, does not mean they put their whole trust in them.

Three: Dreamtelling: An Exercise in Rhetoric

1 Edited by J. Evans and J. H. Whitehouse (Oxford, 1957–9), 3 vols. For the dreams mentioned here see 27 November 1868, 16 October 1869, 7 November 1873 and 7 December 1874.

2 Suras 2, 7, 9.

3 *Journal* (New York, 1952), p. 312.

4 *Books of Memorable Deeds and Sayings*, Book I, 'On dreams', § 7.

5 *Socrates' Daemon*, 13–14.

6 *Antiquities of the Jews*, II, 11–15.

7 *Confessions*, X, 30.

8 See Dorothy Eggan, 'Hopi Dreams in Cultural Perspective', in Grunebaum and Caillois, *The Dream and Human Societies* (Berkeley, 1966), pp. 244–7.

9 *Antiquities of the Jews*, XI, 327.

10 Jill Dubisch, *In a Different Place: Pilgrimage, Gender and Politics at a Greek Island Shrine* (Princeton, NJ, 1996).

11 *Reality and Dream: Psychotherapy of a Plains Indian* (New York, 1969);

see especially pp. 189–90, 251, 425.

12 Schnitzler's dreams are recorded in his *Tagebuch*, 10 vols (Vienna, 1987–2000).

13 *The Interpretation of Dreams*, S.E., IV, p.111.

14 *Introductory Lectures on Psychoanalysis* (1914–16) and *New Introductory Lectures on Psychoanalysis* (1933). The dream quoted here is borrowed from the former, *S.E.*, V, p. 119.

15 *The Interpretation of Dreams*, S.E., V, p. 494.

16 'Approaching the Unconscious', in *Man and his Symbols* (London, 1964), p. 56.

17 *Tagebuch*, vol. V, p. 49.

18 'Approaching the Unconscious', p. 43. Jung thought that the dream was a symbolic representation of a German saying that means 'I do not care what you say about me'.

19 See the various dreams of July 1913, in *Tagebuch*, vol. V, pp. 47–54.

20 *Tagebuch*, vol. VII, p. 338.

21 *The Interpretation of Dreams*, S.E., IV, pp. 204–8.

22 Idem, p. 233.

23 *The Secret Artist: A Close Reading of Sigmund Freud* (London, 2000).

24 Leo Oppenheim, *The Interpretation of Dreams in the Ancient Near East* (Philadelphia, 1956), p. 253.

25 Jean Duvignaud, Françoise Duvignaud, Jean–Pierre Corbeau, *La banque des rêves* (Paris, 1979). The texts quoted here can be found pp. 43 and 55.

26 *La boutique obscure* (Paris, 1973), See especially nos 63 and 101.

27 *Journal* (Hamburg, 1930), see 10 February 1918 and 17 December 1919.

28 Oppenheim, *Dreams in the Ancient Near East*, p. 251.

29 *History of the Jewish War against the Romans*, II, 112.

30 Oppenheim, *Dreams in the Ancient Near East*, p. 253.

31 'On Dreams', II, 17.

Four: Exploring the World of Dream Reports

1 *New Introductory Lectures on Psychoanalysis, S.E.*, XXII, p. 9.

2 *The Diary of a Country Parson*, 5 vols (Oxford, 1921–31), 12 September 1796.

3 These elements, he explained, are called up by the dreamwork when 'there is any psychical reason for making use of them', but he did not expand on the psychic reasons he mentioned. See *The Interpretation of Dreams, S.E.*, IV, p. 237 and 273.

4 *La boutique obscure* (Paris, 1973), no. 52.

5 Henry David Thoreau, *A Week on the Concord and Merrimack Rivers*, Wednesday; in *'Walden' and Other Writings* (Toronto and New York, 1982), p. 75.

6 In a short text dated 1931, *S.E.*, XXI, p. 232.

7 *Dream Power* (New York, 1980) pp. 76, 77, 108.

8 *La boutique obscure*, no. 108.

9 Leo Oppenheim, *The Interpretation of Dreams in the Ancient Near East* (Philadelphia, 1956), p. 227.

10 Flavius Josephus, *Antiquities of the Jews*, XVII, 166.

11 See A. G. McDowell, *Village Life in Ancient Egypt: Laundry Lists and Love Sagas* (Oxford, 2000), doc. no. 81.

12 Quoted by G. E. von Grunebaum, 'The Cultural Function of the Dream as Illustrated by Classical Islam', in Grunebaum and Caillois, eds, *The Dream and Human Societies* (Berkeley, CA, 1966), p. 14.

13 English translation (London, 1949), 20 April 1916.

14 *Memories, Dreams, Reflections* (London, 1961), p. 163.

15 See, for instance, David Fontana's *Teach Yourself to Dream* (London, 1996), p. 26.

16 'Approaching the Unconscious', in *Man and his Symbols* (London, 1964), pp. 51 and 54.

17 Oppenheim, *Dreams in the Ancient Near East*, p. 250.

Five: The Power of Dream Interpreters

1 *History of the Jewish War against the Romans*, II, 112.

2 *My Education: A Book of Dreams* (London, 1995).

3 *Historiae*, 4, 83.

4 For Flavius Josephus see *History of the Jewish War*, op. cit., III, 352– 3. For Artemidorius, *The Interpretation of Dreams*, I, 8–11, IV, 4–6 and 24–6.

5 Ella Sharp, *Dream Analysis* (London, 1937), p. 20.

6 His methods and recommendations are exposed in *The Psychotherapy of Hysteria*, *S.E.*, II, p. 255ff.

7 Sharp, *Dream Analysis*, p. 21.

8 *Therapeutic Consultations in Child Psychiatry* (London, 1971), p. 202.

9 Sharp, *Dream Analysis*, p. 26.

10 'On Beginning the Treatment', *S.E.*, XII, p. 132.

11 Ludwig Edelstein and Emma Edelstein, eds, *Asclepius: A Collection and Interpretation of the Testimonies*, 2 vols (Baltimore, 1945), I, pp. 204–9; II, pp. 148–73.

12 *Five Lectures on Psychoanalysis*, *S.E.*, XI, p. 145.

Conclusion

1 'My Demons: The Legacy', broadcast on BBC 2, 5 September 1992.

Acknowledgements

When I first told my friends and colleagues about my research into dreamtelling, many said: 'Freud has exhausted the topic!' Such a reaction is a significant index of the power of psychoanalysis in our time. But even if Freud has changed our understanding of dreams, there is very little in his work on the way we report them.

At first only Peter Hamilton and Christian Metz were interested in my project; I owe much to Peter for his support and confidence. During the course of writing, the questions raised by Chantal Duchet and Marie-Jeanne Racine proved extremely fruitful. I am much indebted to Giuditta Rosowsky, whose expertise in psychoanalysis and knowledge of Freudian texts as well as of Italian literature were greatly beneficial. I am also obliged to my first readers, Steven Englund and Arnold Rosin. The former was a strict but benevolent censor. The latter has my thankfulness for his patience and attention and for the accuracy of his comments. His keen eye played a decisive part in the completion of this work. Together with dreams already published I have drawn on dreams reported by relatives or friends. I wish to express my gratitude to all those who have shared them with me.

I owe special thanks to the FOCI series editors, whose critical remarks have deeply influenced not only my approach to the topic but also the very conception of this book.

List of Illustrations

p. 121: Gérard Grandville, 'A Walk in the Sky', wood engraving for *Magasin pittoresque* (1857). Author's collection.

p. 129: Handouts for a French dreambook, *La clé des songes* (1904), photography and gouache. Author's collection.

p. 152: Francisco Goya, 'Soplones', plate 48 of *Caprichos, c.* 1795, engraving. Museo del Prado, Madrid (Calcografía). Photo: Museo del Prado.

p. 170: William Blake, 'The Dream of Thiralatha', from a *Large Book of Designs, c.* 1794, colour-painted relief etching finished in pen and watercolour. The British Museum, London (Prints and Drawings). Photo: British Museum.